ACADEMIC WRITING
英語論文の書き方入門

迫 桂＋徳永聡子
Sako Katsura　Tokunaga Satoko

慶應義塾大学出版会

はじめに

　本書の目的は、英語による学術論文作成のための基礎力養成にあり、高等学校修了程度の英語力を有する学習者を対象としています。特に人文学分野での教科書として適しています。

　本書は、英語のアカデミック・ライティングの基盤となる、「英語で書く」ということ、そして「学術的な論文を書く」という2点を柱に据えています。このため論文にふさわしい英語表現や書式、論文の構成や作成法などの実践的な内容に加えて、リサーチの意義や作法といった、学術研究の基礎についても詳述しています。筆者のこれまでの経験に基づきながら、英語論文に初めて取り組む人にも分かりやすいよう、豊富な例と説明を取り入れています。

　アカデミック・ライティングには、次ページの表が示すよう、複数の種類があります。この中でも比較的短めの論文、エッセイ（essay）を書けるようになることが、本書の最終的な目標です。エッセイは日本の大学で課されるレポートに近く、アメリカの大学では term paper や research paper とも称されます。エッセイ・ライティングの学習で培ったことは、他のタイプのアカデミック・ライティングにも応用できます。また、TOEFLやIELTSなど、留学時に必要なライティング試験の対策にも有益でしょう。

　本書は2部構成です。Part 1「英語論文について学ぼう」は理論・準備編で、アカデミック・ライティングの特色や研究の意義、パラグラフの作り方、エッセイの基本構造などについて解説しています。実践編となる Part 2「エッセイを書こう」は、エッセイのトピックを見つけ、構想を練る段階から、リサーチに基づき執筆・完成させるまでを、順を追って説明しています。例文や練習問題を通じて、アカデミック・ライティングの具体例に触れることもできます。また、初学者が陥りやすい問題やその対処法も、適宜紹介しています。本書の各 Chapter（章）を段階的に学び、Appendix（付録）を併用することで、エッセイ完成に至るように構成されています。なお本文の執筆は、Chapters 1、4 (2)、5、6 (2)、7、Appendix を迫が、Chapters 2、3、4 (1、3)、6 (1、3、4) を徳永が担当し、全体を2人で編集しました。

　英語のアカデミック・ライティングの用語には、必ずしも日本語でぴったりする表現があるとは限りません。本書では、適切な日本語のないものや、日本語にすると意味が分かりにくくなってしまうものには、英語表記をそのまま採用しています（例：「coherence」 「thesis statement」）。一方、日本語で適切な表現がある場合は、日本語表記を、カタカナ表記が一般化しているものは、それを採用しています（例：「パラグラフ」「トピック」）。また英語は国や地域によって異なりますが、筆者がイギリス文学を専門とするため、イギリス英語を採用しています。

　本書の完成に至るまでに、たくさんの方々にお世話になりました。英文の作成・チェックをお手伝いくださいました、Andrew Armour氏、Matt Rubinstein氏、Ursula Canton氏、Shazia Jagot氏に心から感謝申し上げます。松田隆美氏、赤江雄一氏からは、執筆の過程で貴重な助言を頂きました。また、慶應義塾大学出版会の石塚礼美氏には、本当にお世話になりました。丁寧で細やかな編集のお仕事に心よりお礼申し上げます。

　アカデミック・ライティングは、「英語で書く」ことだけを目的とした完結的な行為ではありません。本書を通じて「問いを見出し、考え、発信する」という学問の喜びを、一人でも多くの人に味わっていただけたらと願っています。

迫　桂・徳永聡子

参考：アカデミック・ライティングの種類（イギリスのモデル）

Thesis	A very long piece of writing involving personal research for assessment in a PhD course.
Dissertation	A long piece of writing usually involving personal research, written as part of a university degree (Bachelor's or Master's).
Essay	**A relatively short piece of writing dealing with any one subject and usually used to assess coursework.**
Report	An account of a matter given after investigation or consideration. It usually describes something a student has conducted (e.g., an experiment or a survey).
Review / Critique	A description and evaluation of a book, article, film in the light of specific issues and theoretical concerns.
Abstract / Summary	A short and concise description of certain material.
Literature Review	An account (both descriptive and evaluative) of what has been published on a topic by accredited scholars and researchers.

出典：Warwick Skills Programme, University of Warwick, "Academic Writing for Arts & Social Science Students" の教材より。

Table of Contents

はじめに　　　　　　　　　　　　　　　　　　　　　　　i

| PART 1 | 英語論文について学ぼう | 001 |

| CHAPTER 1 | アカデミック・ライティングとは | 003 |

- SECTION 1　アカデミック・ライティングの特色　　005
  - 1-1　主張と論証　　005
  - 1-2　論理性と客観性　　006
  - 1-3　問いの設定　　008
- SECTION 2　剽窃　　008
- SECTION 3　アカデミック・スタイル　　009
- SECTION 4　書式の一貫性　　014
- SECTION 5　英語で書くために　　015
  - 5-1　文法と構文　　015
  - 5-2　英語らしい表現　　016
  - 5-3　辞書を活用しよう　　023
  - 5-4　英語で書かれたものをたくさん読もう　　026

| CHAPTER 2 | パラグラフとは | 029 |

- SECTION 1　パラグラフと Main Idea　　031
- SECTION 2　パラグラフの構造　　033
- SECTION 3　Topic Sentence　　035

Section 4	**Supporting Sentences**	037
	4-1 **Supporting Sentences の役割**	037
	4-2 **Supporting Details**	039
Section 5	**Concluding Sentence**	041
	5-1 **Concluding Sentence の役割**	041
	5-2 **Concluding Sentence を導く便利な表現**	042
Section 6	**Unity と Coherence**	044
	6-1 **Unity**	044
	6-2 **Coherence**	045
Section 7	**Review Exercises**	051

CHAPTER 3　エッセイの構造（1） 057

Section 1	エッセイの3大要素	059
Section 2	パラグラフとエッセイの関係	060
Section 3	エッセイの Unity と Coherence	061
Section 4	モデル・エッセイを読もう	061

PART 2 エッセイを書こう 067

エッセイ作成と調べるプロセス 068

CHAPTER 4 エッセイの枠組みを構想する 069

- SECTION 1 　問いを立てる 071
- SECTION 2 　なぜ「調べる」ことが必要なのか 073
- SECTION 3 　エッセイの骨組みを作成する 075
  - 3-1 　アウトラインとは 075
  - 3-2 　アウトラインの作成方法 076
  - 3-3 　タイトルを考える 079

CHAPTER 5 文献資料の扱い方 081

- SECTION 1 　文献資料について 083
  - 1-1 　どのような文献資料が必要か 083
  - 1-2 　収集した情報の評価 083
  - 1-3 　論証が必要かどうか 084
  - 1-4 　剽窃に注意する 085
- SECTION 2 　文献資料を集める 085
- SECTION 3 　文献資料の情報管理 089
  - 3-1 　情報管理の目的と意義 089
  - 3-2 　情報の記録と管理の方法 089

Section 4	引用	091
4-1	引用の意義と種類	091
4-2	直接引用	092
4-3	間接引用	094
Section 5	出典の示し方	100
5-1	In-Text Citations	100
5-2	Works Cited	102

Chapter 6 エッセイの構造（2） 109

Section 1	Introduction	111
1-1	Introduction の役割と構造	111
1-2	Thesis Statement の重要性	112
1-3	モデル・エッセイの分析	114
1-4	Introduction の作成で注意すべきこと	116
Section 2	Body Paragraphs	118
2-1	Body Paragraphs の役割と構造	118
2-2	エッセイにおける Transition	119
Section 3	Conclusion	125
3-1	Conclusion の役割と構造	125
3-2	Conclusion の作成で注意すべきこと	126
Section 4	Review Exercises	127

Chapter 7 完成に向けて 133

Section 1	書式	135
Section 2	推敲	140
Section 3	チェックリスト	142
Section 4	モデル・エッセイ	144

APPENDIX 153

1. エッセイ作成のスケジュール　155
2. ブレインストーミングのサンプル　156
3. エッセイの構想を練る　158
4. アウトライン　160
5. 文献資料記録ページ　162
6. チェックリスト　164
7. 解答　166

PART 1

英語論文について学ぼう

CHAPTER 1

アカデミック・ライティングとは

SECTION 1　アカデミック・ライティングの特色

　アカデミック・ライティングとは、具体的なトピックに関する主張や見解を、学術的な作法に従いまとめたものです。この礎にあるのが研究（リサーチ）であり、裏を返せば研究の結果をまとめたものといえます。研究とは（特に文系の場合）、自らの知的関心の対象について学問的な問いを立て、それに関する文献資料をできるだけ広く読み、調査や批判的な検討を重ね、問いに対する自分自身の見解を形成していくプロセスすべてを指します。論文というかたちにする時には、対象への知的理解と批判的思考を重ねて導き出した結論を、誰もが理解、検証可能なように、自分の研究分野にふさわしい形式や書式に沿って文章化します。すなわちアカデミック・ライティングとは、**問題を設定するところから、それに対する主張を他者（読み手）に伝えるようアウトプット化するまでの作業すべてを包含します。**

　英語論文の執筆には守るべき決まり事がいろいろあります。学習者の中には、自分の主張が個性的でおもしろければ、そうしたことは二の次と考える人も時々いますが、それは誤解です。よい英語論文を書くためには、まずはアカデミック・ライティングの特質と決まり事を理解する必要があります。

　では、アカデミック・ライティングの特色とは何でしょうか。ここでは、特に重要な3つのポイントを挙げます。

1-1　主張と論証

　研究とは、学問的、知的関心を出発点として問題設定を行い、リサーチによって自己の見解を形成していくことだと述べました。アカデミック・ライティングの究極的な目的は、問いについて自分なりに導き出した主張を、他者に納得して受け入れてもらうところにあります。

　ここでいう主張とは、簡単にいえば意見です。ただし、「○○は△△すべきだ」というタイプのものだけでなく、「○○は△△だ」という見解も含みます。日本人学生が書く論文は、「何がいいたいのかよく分からない」といわれることが多くあります。これは、アカデミック・ライティングの構成要素を理解していないからだけでなく、「意見を提示する」

という意識が不足しているためかもしれません。特に、リサーチをして書く課題の場合、自分の意見を明確にしないまま、調べたことをひたすら説明しがちです。調べ物は、次に述べるように、問いの対象について自分の理解を深め、自分の意見の妥当性を吟味するために行うものです。**論文の主役は、調べ物ではなく、主張です**。

　しかしながら、いかに主張が重要であるといっても、とにかくそれだけを述べ立てればいいわけではありません。主張には、最終的に正しいか、間違っているかを決定することができない内容のものも多くあります。だからこそ、なるべく多くの人に理解してもらえる方法（具体例やデータの提示、専門家の意見の引用など）で、その妥当性を示す必要があるわけです。これを行うプロセスが論証です。

1-2　論理性と客観性

　読み手を納得させるためには、**論理的かつ客観的な論証**が必要です。個人的体験に基づく主張、感情的な主張、論理性のない主張は説得力を持ち得ません。

　例えば、論文で以下の主張を述べるとします。

「1日1個林檎を食べるとインフルエンザ予防に効果がある」

　上記の主張の根拠として、次の2つの事実を挙げたとします。

①「私は昨年の冬、実際に1日1個林檎を食べた」
②「昨年の冬、私は一度もインフルエンザにかからなかった」

この論証の問題は、①と②の因果関係が科学的に示されていないことです。例えば、論者は林檎の他に、インフルエンザ予防に有益となる食べ物を食べたり、運動をしたり、生活パターンを維持していたかもしれません。つまり、①は②という結果に間接的に貢献した可能性はあるかもしれませんが、②という結果に結びつくその他の可能性を一切排除し、①と②の直接的な因果関係を科学的に検証することは困難です。このように、論理が完全に実証され得ない場合、論証は成立しません。

　上記の例のもう1つの問題は、論証の根拠が一般論、個人的経験や見聞によっていて客

観性を欠いていることです。主張に説得力を持たせるためには、適切な事例、資料や文献を用いて論証することが必要です。適切な論証材料とは、客観性が確保された信頼性の高いものです。例えば、「林檎がインフルエンザ予防によい」根拠として、「よくそういわれているから」、「小さい頃に祖母がよくいっていたから」などと主張しても、説得力には欠けます。また、林檎の特産地のポスターに「1日1個のリンゴで風邪知らず！」という宣伝文句があったとしても、それが科学的事実に基づいて書かれたとは限らないので、それを引き合いに出しても強い主張は生まれません。また、匿名個人のブログや存在を確認し得ない団体のウェブサイト上に、林檎の効能を謳う文章があったとしても、書き手が分からなければその情報の信頼性を評価することすらできません。よって、そのような情報を論証材料として用いるのはアカデミックな論文作成でしてはならないことです。一方、権威ある医学学術雑誌に、適切な手順に従って行われた実験で林檎の効能が証明されたという報告がなされていたとしたら、ポスターの宣伝文句や匿名情報よりもずっと高い信頼性があるといえます。情報が氾濫する今日、情報の信頼性を評価・判断することの重要性が高まっていますが、アカデミックな論文を作成する際にも、集めた情報を正確に評価する力が不可欠です。

　主観的で個人的な体験は論証材料にならないと説明しましたが、個人的な体験や身近な事柄をアカデミックな問いに発展させることは大いに可能です。一例を挙げましょう。友人と映画についての感想を交すことを想像してください。感想を述べる場合、「あの映画は嫌い」といい、もし理由を問われれば、「なんとなく。暗いし、とにかく気持ち悪い」と答えることもできます。しかし、学術研究では、「なぜ気持ち悪いという印象を抱くのか」について深く考え、その理由を客観的に説明しようとします。その考察の結果、「この映画が不安感を掻き立てるのは、繰り返し用いられる映像的比喩の効果である」といえば、学術的見解を提示していることになります。さらにこれを論証するには、映像的比喩の例を示し、それが作品中でどれだけ、どのように繰り返されているか説明し、その効果を心理学や精神分析学の視点から分析することができるでしょう。身近な話題については「感想」のレベルで意見を述べることが多いですが、この例から分かるように、より深く掘り下げればアカデミックな論文の考察対象となり得ますし、具体的で客観的な議論が可能な場合も多いのです。

1-3　問いの設定

　以上、問いと主張、論理的で客観的な論証が重要であることを説明してきましたが、実はもう1つ大切な鍵があります。それは、指定された課題の長さで論証が可能な問いを設定することです。自らの知的関心を追求することのみを目的として研究を行う場合は、長さの制限は問題になりません。しかし現実には、何らかの課題として研究を行い、その成果を指定された枠の中で提示するというのが一般的です。その場合、自分が関心を持つトピックが非常に広範なものであったとしても、課題の長さに合わせて焦点を絞り込んでいかねばなりません。例えば、「豊かな人生を送るためにはどうすればよいか」とか「日本の英語教育はどうあるべきか」という問いに関心があったとしても、課題の長さによって議論の対象を制限する必要が生じます。上記1つ目の例であれば、人生の豊かさを左右する要因として住環境に注目し、「大都市の住宅政策においては何が優先されるべきか」と問いを狭めることができるでしょう。また後者の例では、対象を公立小学校の英語教育、しかも、児童の学習動機に絞り、「公立小学校の英語教育において、児童の学習動機をどう高めることができるか」などと問いを設定することができるでしょう。問いと主張の設定は非常に重要ですので、Chapter 4でその手順を詳しく学びます。

アカデミック・ライティング＝「問いの設定→主張+客観的・論理的な論証」

SECTION 2　剽窃

　前のSectionで、アカデミックな世界には決まり事があると述べましたが、最も重要なことが**剽窃の厳禁**です。剽窃とは、他人の著作、意見や見解を盗用することです。英語では **plagiarism** といわれ、その動詞 plagiarise は "to copy another person's ideas, words or work and pretend that they are your own" と説明されています（*Oxford Advanced Learner's Dictionary* (7th ed.)）。日本では、生徒や学生が課題作成時に、出版物やインターネット上の情報をそのまま、しかも、黙って用いる問題が、「コピペ」として取り上げられています。欧米の大学でも、論文作成の作法を学ぶ授業で取り上げるなど、学生の意識

向上のために積極的な方策がとられています。

　剽窃が禁じられているのはなぜでしょうか。1つには、考えや言葉、著作が個人に帰属するからです。音楽や文学作品に著作権があるのと同様、考え、理論、文章、統計情報や実験結果などにも所有権があります。例えば、ある文学作品について批評家が意見を述べていた場合、その意見やそれを表現した文言はその批評家に帰属します。論文を作成する際には、考えや解釈にも所有権があるということを強く意識し、その所有権を尊重せねばなりません。

　剽窃をすべきではないもう1つの理由は、アカデミックな営為の根本にある原理と関わっています。アカデミックな研究の基本となるのは、自ら考えることです。論文を作成する時には、自ら関心があり、意義もあると思われる問いを見つけ、それについて他の人の意見や見解を学び、文献資料を参考にしたりしながら、自分なりの解釈や見解を確立しようと試みます。論文ではそれを「主張」として提示し、その妥当性を示します。コピペに代表される剽窃行為は、このように自ら考える努力を怠り、放棄することです。さらに、アカデミックな営為とは、開かれた議論の場に参加することであり、公共性の高い行為です。情報の共有が活発な議論に欠かせないのと同時に、他人の考えや解釈の所有権は深く尊重せねばなりません。

　剽窃は決してしてはならない行為です。一方で、他人の研究成果や資料に触れることは論文作成に不可欠な要素です。だからこそ、論文で他人の研究成果に言及する場合の決まり事と方法を熟知している必要があります。これらについてはChapter 5で詳しく学びます。

SECTION 3　アカデミック・スタイル

　英語論文を書く際には、言葉や表現に関しても守るべき事柄があります。日本語でも、状況や文脈によって、改まった語彙が使われたり、くだけた表現が使われたりします。同様に、学術論文でも、学術論文に適した語彙や表現の選択がなされます。これはアカデミック・スタイルと呼ばれています。

　アカデミック・スタイルの基本は、客観性、正確さ、分かりやすさです。論文の内容がどれだけ伝わるかは、それを伝える言葉にかかっています。曖昧で、くだけすぎた表現を

使ったのでは、いくらすばらしい内容であっても、高い評価を受けることができません。この意味で、適切な語彙や表現の選択は、学術論文の総合的な質を左右する一要因なのです。

　アカデミック・スタイルは、慣習に依拠する部分が大きいので、確固たる規定があるわけではありません。以下に挙げるのは、広く一般に受け入れられている基本事項です。

アカデミック・スタイルの基本

- I、we、youなどの代名詞は避ける。議論の客観性を担保するために、表現の上で中立的な視点が維持されていることが好ましい。▶ Examples 1, 2, 5, 7 & 8
- 曖昧な表現は避け、正確で意味がはっきりと伝わる表現や語句を用いる。
  ▶ Example 3
- 日常的なくだけた表現や語句は避ける。▶ Examples 3 & 4
- 会話文、スピーチなどに使われる表現や語句は避ける。▶ Examples 5, 6 & 8
- 読み手の想定が正確にできない場合は、読み手を限定するような表現は避ける。
  ▶ Example 7
- 短縮形や省略形は避ける。▶ Examples 9 & 10

　以下に示す例は、2つの文がセットになっています。上の文がアカデミック・スタイルから外れる例で、下がアカデミック・スタイルで書かれた例です。2つの文を比較しながら、アカデミック・スタイルの基本事項を確認しましょう。

Example 1

I think it is good for university students to participate in volunteer work.
▶▶ It is beneficial for university students to participate in volunteer work.

Example 2

The President made an unpopular policy decision. In my opinion, it was necessary.
▶▶ Although the President made an unpopular policy decision, it was necessary.

Example 3

The book is about all sorts of things about Japan.

▶▶ The book discusses various aspects of Japan, including its history, economy, politics, religion and culture.

　3つの例のいずれも、上の文はくだけた印象を読み手に与えます。例えば Example 3 の "all sorts of things" というのは会話でもよく使われる表現で、具体性に欠けます。一方、下の文では、曖昧な表現 "all sorts of things" を、"various aspects of Japan, including its history, economy, politics, religion and culture" と説明していて、より正確かつ具体的です。また、"is about" を "discusses" に置き換えることで、改まった印象を与えます。

Example 4

The company tried to come up with new products, but could not get good ideas. So the company gave up the plan to start business in China. And also the company had to withdraw from the US market because of a bad economy in the US. So it lost a lot of money.

▶▶ The company was unable to launch any new products. It therefore abandoned its plan to enter the Chinese market. In addition, it had to withdraw from the US market due to a recession in the local economy. As a result, the company made a significant loss.

　上の文は、語彙や表現だけでなく、各ポイントをつなぐ接続の仕方も口語的で、全体的にしまりがない印象を与えます。また、代名詞が効果的に使われていません。その結果、the company と the US が繰り返されています。

Example 5

What kind of music do you like? We have our own favourite types of music but there are many kinds of music now. If you go to a music store you will find many kinds of music such as contemporary pop, rock, jazz, R&B, folk and classical music. So you can certainly find your favourite types of music.

▶▶ There is a rich variety of music available today to accommodate different tastes. A visit to a music store will reveal a wide range of music such as contemporary pop, rock, jazz, R&B, folk and classical music.

Example 6

The Japanese women's football team won the world championship. Many people were surprised. Why? People did not think they were strong enough.

▶▶ The Japanese women's football team won the world championship. Many people were surprised, because they had been seen as the underdogs.

　Examples 5 & 6は、疑問文の使い方に問題があります。アカデミック・ライティングにおいて疑問文を避けるべき理由は主に2つあります。1つは、エッセイがスピーチであるかのような印象を与えるということです。スピーチと異なり、ライティングでは読者に「呼びかける」必要はありません。具体的にいえば、youやweという代名詞は登場する必要がないはずです。もう1つの理由は、議論の流れを文で説明する代わりに疑問文を使った場合、問答か会話文のような印象を与えるということです。

Example 7

In Japan it was usual that women stopped working when they married. But now more and more women continue working after they marry and have children. But there is not enough help for working parents. So they are constantly stressed under the pressure of juggling work and family. What should we do about this? What can each of us do to help them? We have to cooperate to make Japan a family-friendly country. The local governments, NPOs, volunteer groups and organisations have suggested many solutions.

▶▶ In Japan it was usual for women to stop working when they married, but now more and more women continue working after they marry and have children. Yet there is not enough help for working parents and they are therefore constantly stressed, trying to juggle work and family. Local governments, NPOs, volunteer groups and organisations have suggested various solutions to improve the situation so that a career and a happy family life can both be attainable.

　この例でも不要な疑問文が使われています。スピーチであれば、聞き手を惹きつける方法として有効ですが、ライティングでは好ましいとはいえません。また、この例では、"we"という代名詞が使われています。これは、読み手を日本人または日本に住む人と書き手が想定していることを示しています。確かに、読み手を想定することは重要です。また、日本の大学生が授業の課題で英語のエッセイを書く場合は、読み手を日本人と想定することが自然に感じられるかもしれません。しかし一般的には、正確に想定ができない場合はあえて読み手を限定した書き方は避けるべきです。下の文から分かるように、表現を工夫すれば、読み手の限定を排除し、中立的な視点で書くことが十分可能です。

Example 8

As I have shown, doing a little exercise every day is good for preventing obesity. If you want to lose weight, you should do exercise. Let's exercise to lose weight!

▶▶　As has been explained, a brief daily exercise is effective for preventing obesity. It is recommended that anyone concerned about their weight should take exercise.

　上の文の "Let's exercise to lose weight!" は、まるでスピーチの締めの呼びかけのようです。スピーチでは熱弁も説得力の一部となりますが、論文では感嘆符（exclamation mark）を使うような呼びかけ式の説得は行いません。

Example 9

It won't be the same again.

▶▶　It will not be the same again.

Example 10

A recent survey by Japan Telecom has revealed that 27% of children between the ages of 7 and 12 own a mobile.

▶▶　A recent survey by Japan Telecom has revealed that 27% of children between the ages of 7 and 12 own a mobile phone.

論文では改まった表現が好ましいとされていますので、短縮形や略語は用いません。

> **ONE POINT ADVICE** 実は、著名な研究者が書いた文章で、ここに挙げたアカデミック・スタイルの決まりを守っていないものがあります。これは深い見識を有し、独自の表現スタイルを持つ経験豊富な書き手だからこそ受け入れられることといえます。しかし、論文作成法そのものを学ぶ過程にある場合、いろいろと自己のスタイルを実験する前に、まずは基本を身につけることが大事でしょう。

SECTION 4 書式の一貫性

　論文の情報を正確に伝える上で、一貫して統一された書式は非常に重要です。そのため、アカデミックな世界では書式について指定があることが一般的です。書式の方式には標準的に使われているものが複数あり、どれを採用するかは、学問領域や学術雑誌、大学・研究機関によって異なります。いずれも、ページ設定から、文献資料の引用の仕方、出典の示し方、参考文献リストの作成方法、表記の仕方まで、論文作成全般に関して詳細に規定しています。

　本書では、アメリカ学術団体 MLA（Modern Language Association）が定めた MLA 方式を採用しています。母体はアメリカの団体ですが、アメリカ国内に限らず、人文学の分野でたいへん広範にわたり使用されています。本書の Chapter 5 は、引用の方法、出典明示の方法、文献資料リスト作成の方法を説明しています。Chapter 7 は、書式の基本的な事項を説明しています。ただし、すべての規則をここで紹介することはできませんので、詳細な情報は、*MLA Handbook for Writers of Research Papers* の最新版（2014 年 1 月現在、第 7 版が最新版）を参照してください。また、アメリカの Purdue 大学が開発運営しているオンラインサイトでも、MLA 方式について丁寧に説明されています[★1]。本書の説明の大部分は、そこで公開されている MLA Formatting and Style Guide と *MLA Handbook* を典拠としています。

書式の一部として、英語論文では語彙やスペリングにも一貫性を持たせることが大切です。英語は話されている地域によって、語彙や表現、スペリングのシステムが大きく異なります。例えば、アメリカで使われる英語とイギリスで使われる英語は、アメリカ英語とイギリス英語として区別されています。具体的な例を挙げると、同じ動詞でもアメリカ英語では -ize、イギリス英語では -ise と表記されます。語彙やスペリングのシステムについて指定がない場合は、基本的にどの地域の英語を用いてもよいとされています。ただし、論文の最初から終わりまで一貫していなければなりません。本書で採用している MLA 方式も、どの地域の英語を用いるかについては規定していませんが、スペリングは一貫していなければならないと指摘しています。ただし、文献資料の情報を原文のまま引用する場合は、原文のスペリングや語彙を変更してはいけません（詳しくは Chapter 5 を参照のこと）。

　語彙やスペリングのシステムに詳しくない場合、同一のシステムを基準にした辞書を揃えて使用すれば、論文を書く際に語彙やスペリングの一貫性を保つ助けになるでしょう。

SECTION 5　英語で書くために

5-1　文法と構文

　昨今の英語教育では、英語のコミュニケーション能力を強調する傾向が強いようです。さらに、「コミュニケーション＝スピーキング力、会話力」ととらえられがちです。記憶一辺倒で「使えない」受験英語に対する反動も相まって、「ブロークンでも積極的に話すことが大事」「英語が立派かどうかより、話す内容が大事」であるとか、「熱意をもって話せば、いいたいことは伝わる」とよくいわれます。もちろん、休暇旅行中であれば、「ブロークン」英語でも意思疎通を図り、用事を足し、地元の人と交流をする経験ができたのならば、それは大きな自信と喜びになります。また、お互いに旅行者で時間に余裕がある者同士なら、つたない英語でも、見知らぬ土地から来た人間の話に辛抱強く耳を傾けてくれる

★1　Russell, Tony, Allen Brizee, and Elizabeth Angeli. "MLA Formatting and Style Guide." *The Purdue OWL*. Purdue U Writing Lab, 4 Apr. 2010. Web. 3 Sep. 2011.

かもしれません。しかし、英語の正確さがそれほど重要ではない場面がある一方、正確さが重要な場合も多くあります。アカデミック・ライティングも後者に該当します。随筆ではありませんから、「ブロークン」でも情熱をもって書き連ねればよい、という方針は通用しません。文法などの基礎力がなければ、学術的な議論を構築することは不可能です。ただ話せばよい、書けばよい、ということではなく、正しい文章で論理的な議論を構築する、これを会得するためには、文法や構文の完全習得と再確認を繰り返すことが必須です。

　正しい文法・構文の知識に不安のある人は、論文執筆に取り組む前に、下に挙げた参考書などを活用して必ず復習してください。また実際の執筆段階に入っても、自分の文法や構文が正しい理解に基づいているのか、迷う時があると思います。少しでも覚束ない時は、面倒に思わず、参考書や辞書を引いて確認する習慣をつけましょう。参考書の目次や索引は文法項目ごとになっていますし、具体的な用法や語句（例えば "will" と "be going to" の用法の差）から調べることもできます。こうした確認を怠ってしまうと、同じ間違いをずっと繰り返し続けてしまいますので、早い段階に文法の復習をしましょう。

◎ 有益な文法書など ◎

- Hewings, Martin. *Advanced Grammar in Use with Answers*. 3rd ed. Cambridge: Cambridge UP, 2013. Print.
- Murphy, Raymond. *English Grammar in Use with Answers: A Self-Study Reference and Practice Book for Intermediate Students of English*. 4th ed. Cambridge: Cambridge UP, 2012.
- Swan, Michael. *Practical English Usage*. 3rd ed. Oxford: Oxford UP, 2005. Print.（マイケル・スワン『オックスフォード実例現代英語用法辞典〈第3版〉』吉田正治訳（東京：研究社、2007））
- Swan, Michael, and Catherine Walter. *How English Works: A Grammar Practice Book*. Oxford: Oxford UP, 1997. Print
- 安藤貞雄『現代英文法講義』（東京：開拓社、2005）

5-2　英語らしい表現

　文法的に誤りがない文章でも、英語の表現として不自然だったり、間違っていることが

少なくありません。これは多くの場合、日本語で考えたことをそのまま英語に置き換えていることに起因するようです。しかし、機械的に英語を当てはめるだけでは、英語として自然な文が成り立ちません。翻訳ソフトを使った英作文がしばしば不自然で無益なのも同じ理由からです。英語らしい表現を生み出すためには、英語で考える、つまり、思考を英語的なものにするとよいとよくいわれます。筆者たちもこのような考え方に賛同しますが、これは継続的な努力と時間を要することです。一方、典型的な誤りを知っておけば、それに注意して論文を書くことができます。よって、この Section では、日本語を主に使用する人に共通してみられる表現の問題を以下に取り上げます。

同じ単語、表現、文章構造を繰り返す。 日本語と比べ、英語では、語句の置き換えや表現の言い換えによって、繰り返しを避けます。

> **Examples**

★ 繰り返しの多い悪い例

1. There are many things that every family can do to reduce energy consumption at home. One of the most effective ways of reducing energy consumption is to use air-conditioning less. Another way of reducing energy consumption is to reduce the amount of water they use while taking a shower. . . . Some people argue that to use air-conditioning less may harm people's health. . . . As these examples show, there are many things that every family can do to reduce energy consumption at home.

2. The company did business in the US and it was successful. But before it started business in the US, it did many things to ensure the success of their business. First of all, it had to create new products for the local market. To determine what kinds of products were in demand, it did an extensive market survey. Once it decided the new line of products, they started wide-ranging marketing activities.

★ 言い換えをした良い例

3. Andy Warhol produced many works which in many ways were opposed to traditional

classical art. He was also a celebrity as much as he was an artist and was often featured in the media for his provoking comments and unconventional behaviour. Many, however, admired this eccentric and volatile artist.

日本語をそのまま英語に翻訳したような表現。

上の文が不自然な表現を含んだ例で、下の文が英語らしい表現に変更したものです。

Examples

1. Although the global financial crisis existed, the country was not as severely affected as its neighbours.
    ▶▶ Although there was a global financial crisis, the country was not as severely affected as its neighbours.

日本語の「～がある（あった）」という表現にひかれて、"exist" という単語を用いるケースがありますが、"happen/take place" といった動詞（句）や "there is" という構文のほうが自然なことがあります。

2. There was a free journalist at the crime scene.
    ▶▶ There was a freelance journalist at the crime scene.

「フリー・ジャーナリスト」は和製英語です。

3. That topic was the main of the meeting.
    ▶▶ That was the main topic of the meeting.

日本語でいう「メイン」と異なり、英語では単独で使われません。"Main" という単語は名詞の前に置かれ、名詞を修飾する形容詞です。

4. In the last World Cup Tournament the Japanese team fought with the England team.
    ▶▶ In the last World Cup Tournament the Japanese team played against the England team.

「戦う」といっても、文脈によって動詞を使いわける必要があります。また、日本語の「○○と戦う」という表現にひきずられて "with" が使われているのも誤りです。

5. He challenged the entrance examination to the top national university.
   ▶▶ He attempted the entrance examination to the top national university.

日本語で「チャレンジする」というと「大変な課題や試練に挑む」「ためしに何かをする」という意味になりますが、英語では、(1) "to question whether a statement or an action is right, legal, etc.; to refuse to accept sth" (2) "to invite sb to enter a competition, fight, etc.; to suggest strongly that sb should do sth" (3) "to test sb's ability and skills, especially in an interesting way" (*Oxford Advanced Learner's Dictionary* (7th ed.)) などの意味になります。また英語では "a challenging task" のように形容的に使われることもあります。

6. The price was expensive.
   ▶▶ The price was high.

日本語の「高い」と「値段が高い」を混同している例も多く見かけます。「○○が高い（低い、多い、少ない）」と英語でいう場合、○○の内容によって違う単語が使われます。

日本語の定義で同じ語を混同して、間違った意味で使っている。

Examples

1. 「許す」「認める」

   The student was permitted to the university.
   ▶▶ The student was accepted by the university.

2. 「要求する」「必要とする」

   John demanded wheelchair access.
   ▶▶ John required wheelchair access.

3. 「職業」「仕事」

　She was looking for a profession.

　▸▸ She was looking for a job.

4. 「面白く思う」「関心がある」

　He was intrigued by philosophy.

　▸▸ He was interested in philosophy.

5. 「一風変わった」「特有の」

　The country has a peculiar culture.

　▸▸ The country has a unique culture.

従属接続詞の誤った使い方。特に、Because、While、Althoughなどを独立文の文頭に用いる誤りが多く見受けられます。

Examples

1. Many people opposed the plan to build a new motorway outside the town. Because it was expected to cut through a beautiful stretch of green fields which the local people cherished.

　▸▸ Many people opposed the plan to build a new motorway outside the town because it was expected to cut through a beautiful stretch of green fields which the local people cherished.

　または

　▸▸ Many people opposed the plan to build a new motorway outside the town. This was because it was expected to cut through a beautiful stretch of green fields which the local people cherished.

2. The first group of students achieved high scores in their examinations. While the second group performed poorly.

▶▶ The first group of students achieved high scores in their examinations, while the second group performed poorly.

▶▶ The first group of students achieved high scores in their examinations. By contrast, the second group performed poorly.

または

▶▶ The first group of students achieved high scores in their examinations. However, the second group performed poorly.

3. The plan was dismissed. Although it was believed to be an effective way to attract new businesses to the area.

▶▶ The plan was dismissed, although（または、despite the fact that）it was believed to be an effective way to attract new businesses to the area.

And、butなどの等位接続詞の誤った使い方。等位接続詞で文を始めたり、そのすぐ後にコンマをつけない。

Examples

1. He bought a former factory building in 1954. And he converted it into modern flats.
    ▶▶ He bought a former factory building in 1954 and converted it into modern flats.

2. She was a very popular candidate. But she was not elected.
    ▶▶ Although she was a very popular candidate, she was not elected.

3. It was raining heavily, but, he did not mind.
    ▶▶ It was raining heavily, but he did not mind.

4. He always enjoyed cooking. So, he became a chef.
    ▶▶ Since he always enjoyed cooking, he became a chef.

> 🔒 **接続詞のポイント**
>
> 等位接続詞は、同等の2つのものをつなげる役割があり、2つの独立節をつなぐことができます。しかし、それぞれの独立節の内容の重要性が同等でない場合、2つの内容に因果関係など何らかの関係性がある場合は、従属接続詞を用いてそれを明確にします。

自動詞と他動詞の誤った区別。不安な場合は、辞書を使って確認しましょう。

Examples

1. The committee discussed about the proposal.
   ►► The committee discussed the proposal.

2. The train reached to Tokyo.
   ►► The train reached Tokyo.

3. The school considered about the complaints from the parents.
   ►► The school considered the complaints from the parents.

時制や人称の不一致。代名詞の使い方は特に重要です（詳しくは**Chapter 2**を参照）。

Examples

1. Mr Cain stated that he intends to take a more eco-friendly approach.
   ►► Mr Cain stated that he intended to take a more eco-friendly approach.

2. He argued that Mrs Hornby's idea is good.
   ►► He argued that Mrs Hornby's idea was good.

3. The Education Minister agreed to review the problems and to seek professional advice to solve it.
   ▶▶ The Education Minister agreed to review the problems and to seek professional advice to solve them.

冠詞の誤った使い方。日本語話者にとって冠詞を使い分けるのは難しいといわれています。文脈に合わない冠詞を使っているケースだけでなく、冠詞が脱落しているケースも多いようです。

Examples

1. Computer has become part of modern life.
   ▶▶ The computer/Computers has/have become part of modern life.

2. The head teacher was keen on modernising school and introduced new evaluation system.
   ▶▶ The head teacher was keen on modernising the school and introduced a new evaluation system.

◎ 便利な冠詞辞典 ◎
・樋口昌幸、マイケル・ゴーマン『例解 現代英語冠詞事典』（東京：大修館書店、2003）

5-3　辞書を活用しよう

　文法的に正しく、英語として自然な表現で書くためには、辞書を正しく活用することが大切です。英作文の授業などで、和英辞書は使うなと指導された人もいるかもしれません。その意図するところは、ある日本語の単語を和英辞書で引いて、ただ英単語に置き換えただけでは、日本語の語感で考えていた内容にはなり得ないということです。一方で初学者の場合、自由に使える英単語や表現の数にも限りがあります。ですから自分の知っている

英単語だけを駆使しようとしても、それには限界があるでしょう。では、具体的にはどのように辞書を活用すればいいのでしょうか。

ⓐ 類義語辞典・連語辞書を使う

　似た意味の別な表現を調べるためには、類義語辞典を活用すると、和英辞典だけに頼るよりも表現の幅がずっと広がります。英語の類義語辞典を利用すれば、日本語を挟まないので、微妙な意味の違いから見当はずれな単語を探し当ててしまう可能性も低くなります。特に論文で文献資料の要約や言い換えを行う際にも大活躍します（要約と言い換えについては、Chapter 5 で詳説します）。代表的な類義語辞典としては、*Roget's International Thesaurus* (Collins Reference) や *Random House Roget's College Thesaurus* (Random House) などがあります。

　また単語同士の結びつきのパターンを押さえることも重要です。これはコロケーションと呼ばれます。コロケーション辞典では、ある特定の名詞がどのような動詞や形容詞と一緒に使われるのかを、用例とともに確認することができます。市川繁治郎編『新編 英和活用大辞典』（研究社）や *Oxford Collocations Dictionary for Students of English* (Oxford UP) の使用をお薦めします。

Practice ①

1. Using an English thesaurus, find as many words as possible which are exchangeable with "say" in the following sentence.

   Mrs Parker says that many schools will suffer from the deep cuts in government funding.

2. What verbs can be used to mean "do" business?

ⓑ 英英辞典を使う（意味と語法を確認し、例を参照する）

　和英辞典や類義語辞典で候補となる語をいくつか見つけたとしましょう。ここで、最初

のほうに挙げられている語を自動的に選んだりしてはいけません。なぜなら、その単語が文脈に合うとは限らず、伝えたい意味と微妙に異なる意味を持っている可能性があるためです。そこで、英英辞典を使い、候補の単語を調べます。その際、単語の定義だけでなく、**例文**にも目を通し、その単語が自分が意図する意味を持つかどうかを判断します。また、その単語を正しく使えるように、**語法**も確認します。この作業を怠ると、文法的には誤りでなくても、意味が通じなかったり、英語として不自然な表現を生み出す可能性が高くなります。

　英和辞典よりも英英辞典が好ましいのは、細かなニュアンスの違いを豊富な用例や説明でつかめるからです。特に、日本語では同じような意味を持つ単語の違いを理解するのに大変便利です。また、単語の意味を英語のまま理解する習慣をつけると、英文を読む時にいちいち日本語に翻訳するプロセスを排除できますし、その単語を用いて自然な表現を作りやすくもなります。

　さまざまな英英辞典がありますが、英語を母国語としない学習者向けの辞書としては、*Collins Cobuild English Dictionary* (Collins)、*Longman Dictionary of Contemporary English* (Longman) などが、またもう少し上級者向けのものとしては、*Macmillan English Dictionary for Advanced Learners* (Macmillan)、*Oxford Advanced Learner's Dictionary* (Oxford UP)、*Random House Webster's Unabridged Dictionary* (Random House) などが良いでしょう。

Example

peculiarとunique

　両単語とも、英和で調べると、「独特の、特有の、固有の」と似た意味を持つように思えます。しかし、英英辞典で調べるとニュアンスの差が明らかになります。

- peculiar: strange or unusual, especially in a way that is unpleasant or worrying (*Oxford Advanced Learner's Dictionary* (7th ed.))
- unique: being the only one of its kind; very special or unusual (*Oxford Advanced Learner's Dictionary* (7th ed.))

Practice 2

Look up the following sets of words in an English-English dictionary and find out differences in their meanings.

1. smart, clever, bright, wise
2. have, possess, own
3. obtain, get, acquire, attain
4. personal, private

Practice 3

The underlined words in the following sentences do not fit in the context. Find more appropriate words for each.

1. It is sure that the event will be very successful.
2. Teenage children can be very delicate with how they are perceived by their peers.
3. Children should be taught not to desert food.

5-4 英語で書かれたものをたくさん読もう

　書くために読む、というと不思議に思われるかもしれませんが、表現力を伸ばすためには、読むことがとても重要です。なぜなら、読むことで、頭の引出しに語彙と表現が豊富に蓄えられていき、書く時にそれを取り出して使うことができるからです。何もないところから、優れた表現や言い回しが出てくるはずはありません。読むことで、自分の英語の引き出しにサンプルを増やしていくのです。

　お薦めの1つの方法は、常にノートを持ち歩いて、新たに学んだ表現や気になった言い回しをメモし、機会を見つけては実際に使ってみることです。学びたい言語に日常的に接する努力はもちろん大切ですが、より意識すべきことは、アンテナを張って言葉への感覚を日頃から研ぎすますことです。自分の論文にふさわしい表現は、当然のことながら、読むべき参考資料の中にたくさん見つかります。研究を進めてさまざまな資料を読むうちに、キーワードとなる言葉や表現に繰り返し出会うでしょう。そうした言葉に敏感になり、実際の論文でも使っていくのです。つまり英語の表現を借りる、「英借文」をすることが、英語の文章作成上達への秘訣といえます。

　さらに学術論文で使う英語表現には、ある程度定型化されたものもあります。また昨今の英語教育では、English for Academic Purposes（学術目的のための英語）という分野

が発達し、学術用の単語・表現習得に特化した問題集なども刊行されています。そうした基本語彙をマスターするのも有益でしょう。

◎ 表現集など ◎
・崎村耕二『英語論文によく使う表現』（東京：創元社、1991）
・安原和也『英語論文基礎表現717』（東京：三修社、2011）
・McCarthy, Michael, and Felicity O'Dell. *Academic Vocabulary in Use with Answers*. Cambridge: Cambridge UP, 2008. Print.
・Schmitt, Diane, and Norbert Schmitt. *Focus on Vocabulary: Mastering the Academic Word List*. White Plains: Pearson ESL, 2005. Print.

CHAPTER 2

パラグラフとは

Chapter 1で説明したように、アカデミック・ライティングでは、設定した問いに対する答えを「主張 + 論証」から成る議論で提示します。この時、議論を構成する論点を1つずつ分かりやすく、論理的一貫性を保ちながら説明する必要があります。具体的には、パラグラフ（paragraph）を基礎単位として議論を展開させます。

　日本人が作成した文章は、主張がぼやけて曖昧だと指摘されることがよくあります。それは多くの場合、パラグラフの基本構造の理解不足に起因するようです。どれだけ立派な主張や見解を持っていたとしても、また文法や構文が正確な文を書いても、パラグラフの構造を押さえていないと、読み手を説得させる文章にはなり得ません。また、エッセイはパラグラフが論理的に組み立てられたもので、両者の構造は類似しています（詳細はChapter 3で学びます）。このため、パラグラフの理解なしには、エッセイを書く道筋は立てられないといっても過言ではないでしょう。そこでこのChapterでは、良いエッセイを書くための第一歩として、パラグラフについて学びます。

SECTION 1　パラグラフとMain Idea

　パラグラフとは、論理的に構成された文（sentence）の集まりです。日本語では「段落」といわれますが、パラグラフと「段落」に内包される概念は完全に一致するわけではありません。日本語で文章を書く場合、文章の長さのバランスを取ったり、リズムを整え、効果的な強調を行うために、段落という区切りが使われることがよくあります。しかし、英語のアカデミック・ライティングにおけるパラグラフは、内容と形式単位が密接に関わっています。

　パラグラフにおいて特に重要なのは、**1つのパラグラフでは、限定されたトピック（topic）1つについて、1つの主張のみを述べる**という点です。このパラグラフにおける主張は、**main idea**と呼ばれています。パラグラフ内のすべての文は、main ideaにつながり、読み手がそれを理解するのに有効でなければなりません。つまり、パラグラフは単なる文の集合体ではなく、main ideaを分かりやすく、説得力を持って伝えることを目的として、複数の文が積み重なったものなのです。

> 🔒 **パラグラフの鉄則**
>
> 1つのパラグラフで扱うトピックは1つ、それに関する main idea も1つ！

Example

次のパラグラフは上の基本を守ることができていません。その理由を考えましょう。

Ⓐ　Geoffrey Chaucer's *The Canterbury Tales* is a collection of stories told in a variety of styles within the broader framing story of a group of pilgrims who enter into a story-telling competition as they travel to Canterbury Cathedral together. It is similar in some respects to Giovanni Boccaccio's *The Decameron*, which tells of ten travellers escaping the plague-ridden city of Florence, who pass the time on their journey by telling tales to each other, totalling one hundred tales over ten days, with four days for chores and worship. Ⓑ Also, *One Thousand and One Nights* or *The Arabian Nights* is a collection of stories told by Scheherazade, the new bride of a king who believes all women are untrustworthy and puts all of his wives to death at dawn after the wedding night. The clever and inventive Scheherazade postpones her own execution for one thousand and one nights by telling the king an elaborate story that remains unfinished at sunrise, and turns into a new story the following evening. Ⓒ The world's longest-running soap opera was *Guiding Light*, which ran on NBC and CBS radio from 1937 to 1956 and on CBS television from 1952 to 2009, for a total of 18,262 episodes. The oldest soap opera still running is *The Archers*, which has been broadcast on BBC radio since 1950 and reached its 16,470th episode on 19 July 2011.

このパラグラフの冒頭Ⓐでは、チョーサーの『カンタベリー物語』という作品が、カン

タベリーに向かう巡礼者たちの語るおはなしを寄せ集めたものであること（第1文）、そして、それがボッカッチョの『デカメロン』の枠組みと類似していると述べています（第2文）。次の部分Ⓑでは、『千夜一夜物語（アラビアンナイト）』という、結婚式の翌日の明け方までに新しく迎えた花嫁を次々と死に追いやる王に、毎晩おはなしを語る王妃の物語を説明しています。そして最後の箇所Ⓒでは、アメリカとイギリスの長寿メロドラマ番組『ガイディング・ライト』と『アーチャーズ』の放送年数とエピソード数を説明しています。

　一見すると、Ⓐ、Ⓑ、Ⓒは互いに関連のある内容のように思えるかもしれません。しかし、いずれも事実を述べているだけで、何かを論じているわけではありません。物語集というキーワードで、3種類の作品について説明しているだけで、すべてに共通する論点もありません。つまり、このパラグラフには main idea が欠けています。ゆえにアカデミック・ライティングのパラグラフとしては、これは不合格なのです。

　では、どのようにすれば main idea を打ち出し、一貫した論のあるパラグラフを作成することができるのでしょうか。次の Section からは、main idea を核としてパラグラフがどのように構成されているのか、また各構成要素がいかなる働きを担っているのか、具体例を検討しながら解説していきます。

SECTION 2　パラグラフの構造

　Section1 で学んだように、パラグラフでは、1つのトピックとそれに関する main idea を1つだけ提示します。1つの main idea を述べることによって、パラグラフ内の論理的統一が保たれます。もし2つ以上の主張があるならば、新しいパラグラフを作成しなくてはいけません。パラグラフの長さについて具体的な決まりはありませんが、あまりに長すぎる場合は2つ以上のトピックが1つのパラグラフ内に混在していないか、また短すぎる場合は、トピックが適切な大きさか、あるいは他のパラグラフと一緒にまとめる方がよいのではないか、文章を再検討する必要があります。

　パラグラフは、次の3つの要素から構成されています。

> 🔒 **パラグラフの基本構造**
>
> **1. Topic sentence**
>   パラグラフのトピックを示し、それについての書き手のmain ideaを提示する。
>
> **2. Supporting sentences**
>   1で述べたmain ideaを読み手に納得させるために、その説明や内容の補強を行う。
>
> **3. Concluding sentence**
>   パラグラフの終了を知らせ、main ideaを別の言葉で述べる、あるいは全体の要旨をまとめる。

　上記3つの要素がパラグラフを構成し、論理的一貫性を保ちつつ「主張（main idea）＋論証」を展開させる役目を果たしています。
　それでは、上に挙げたパラグラフの3つの要素を意識しながら、下のモデル・パラグラフを読みましょう（各要素については、次のSection以降で詳説します）。

Model Paragraph 1

A Topic sentence

　　Many languages contain words that are said to be untranslatable and are a source of pride for the culture that created them. For example, the German *schadenfreude* can be translated literally as "shameful joy," but more properly means the feeling of joy experienced at another person's failure. The French *esprit d'escalier* is "the wit of the staircase"—a clever response or retort that you think of only when it is too late. More difficult to translate is the Portuguese *saudade*, which is said to refer to a vague and constant desire or longing for something that does not exist, and perhaps will never exist. In Brazil there is a national day of *saudade*, reflecting the importance of the word and the concept to their culture. Similarly, *sisu* represents a

B Supporting sentences

uniquely Finnish kind of toughness and stoicism, *hygge* is a warm and cosy feeling felt only by the Danish people, and *lagom* is the Swedish word for the sensible moderation of the Swedes. Most elusive, perhaps, is the Spanish *duende*, a heightened state of emotion, authenticity, spirit and playfulness. Although the sense of these words may be learned by speakers of other languages, they are not easily translatable: they may take a sentence or a paragraph or even a whole page to convey. Such words are an invaluable part of the language and culture that produced them.

C — Concluding sentence

SECTION 3 Topic Sentence

　Main idea（トピックに関する書き手の主張や見解）を述べるセンテンスは **topic sentence** と呼ばれ、一般的に、パラグラフの冒頭に置かれます。パラグラフの要点あるいは結論を topic sentence によって最初に提示することで、読み手にパラグラフの目的や意図、方向性を示します。

　モデル・パラグラフ（1）では、第 1 文（二重下線部）が topic sentence です。この第 1 文でパラグラフ全体のトピックである「言語」"languages"（あるいは "many languages"）が提示されています。そして筆者は、「言語」"languages" には、それを生み出した文化的な差異ゆえに翻訳することのできない性質がある（". . . contain words that are said to be untranslatable and are a source of pride for the culture that created them"）という、トピックに関する自身の見解を述べています。

　良い topic sentence は、パラグラフの要点を的確に伝えます。Topic sentence の内容が広すぎたり、漠然としていると、パラグラフの内容を読み手は正確に把握することができません。また限定的だったり、詳細すぎてもいけません。なぜなら具体的な内容の提示や補強を次の supporting sentences で行うからです。Topic sentence だけで完結してしまうと、パラグラフとして展開させることができなくなります。同様に、単にトピックの紹介や感想、事実を述べただけでは topic sentence になりません。Topic sentence は、議論の展開を可能にするものでなくてはなりません。適切な大きさのトピックを設定し、そ

れについての自分の見解をしっかり定めることが肝要です。

　さらに、1つのパラグラフでは1つのトピックだけを扱い、そこに盛り込まれるmain ideaも1つだけという、パラグラフの鉄則を思い出しましょう。例えば下の3つめの例文には、2つのmain ideasが含まれています。これでは2つのパラグラフの内容になってしまいます。このような場合、自分がパラグラフで最も述べたいことは何かを再検討し、main ideaを1つに絞りましょう。

Topic Sentenceの良い例・悪い例

- There are three benefits associated with school uniforms in the Japanese education system. ○

- School uniforms reflect aspects of Japanese culture. ✕
  ▶▶ 1つのパラグラフで扱うには大きすぎる

- The Japanese school uniform goes back to the Meiji era and wearing a school uniform is a breach of a child's right to individuality and self-expression. ✕
  ▶▶ トピックとmain ideaが複数ある

- The school uniform of my high school is very cute. ✕
  ▶▶ 感想に留まっている

🔒 **Topic Sentence のポイント**

・パラグラフのトピックとそれに関する書き手のmain ideaを提示する。
・パラグラフの冒頭（特に第1文）に置かれることが多い。
・内容は広すぎず、狭すぎず。
・議論の余地がない主観的な感想や単なる事実を述べない。

Practice 1

1. For the following paragraph, choose the best topic sentence from among a, b and c.

_____ In the learning process students need to relate new pieces of information to their previous knowledge in order to make it meaningful. In other words, they have to construct their own knowledge. If students fail to engage in this process, the new information remains isolated and meaningless to them. As a result, they will forget it quickly. Because this active engagement requires time and effort, it is unlikely that unmotivated students will engage in this process. Therefore, motivation is considered to be essential for successful, active learning.

(a) To be successful learners, students should be motivated and devote themselves to their own subjects.
(b) Motivation is a prerequisite for learning because it is essential for a student's active engagement with new information.
(c) Constructing knowledge is the most significant process because it registers new learning in one's own memory.

SECTION 4　Supporting Sentences

4-1　Supporting Sentencesの役割

　Topic sentence で提示した main idea を読み手に納得してもらうためには、具体例を示したり、説明を加えて、論拠を挙げる必要があります。これは main idea の内容をサポートするものなので、**supporting points** と呼ばれます。そして supporting points を提示する文章を、**supporting sentences** といいます。モデル・パラグラフ（1）を例に、topic sentence と supporting points がどのように関係しているか分析してみましょう。
　このパラグラフでは、第1文、"Many languages contain words that are said to be

untranslatable and are a source of pride for the culture that created them" が topic sentence でした。続く supporting sentences では複数の言語の具体例を引き合いに出して、main idea として述べたことを立証しています。

- the German *schadenfreude*. . . .
- The French *esprit d'escalier*. . . .
- the Portuguese *saudade*. . . .
- *sisu* represents a uniquely Finnish kind of toughness and stoicism. . . .
- *hygge* is a warm and cosy feeling felt only by the Danish people. . . .
- *lagom* is the Swedish word. . . .
- the Spanish *duende*. . . .

このように、topic sentence に続く supporting sentences で、具体例を挙げたり、説明や理由を加えることで、main idea を支える supporting points を示し、書き手の主張に説得力を持たせます。モデル・パラグラフ(1)の場合、第2文（For example, the German *schadenfreude*. . . .）から第7文（Most elusive, perhaps, is the Spanish *duende*. . . .）で具体例を挙げ、パラグラフの main idea を例証しているのです。エッセイにおける main idea と supporting points の関係は、次のように図示できます。

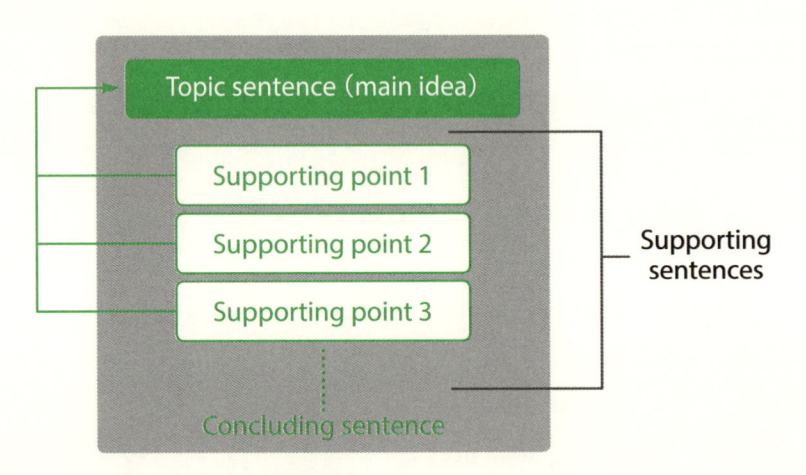

```
┌─────────────────────────────────────────┐
│     Topic sentence (main idea)          │
│                                         │
│        Supporting point 1               │  ┐
│                                         │  │ Supporting
│        Supporting point 2               │  │ sentences
│                                         │  │
│        Supporting point 3               │  ┘
│                                         │
│        Concluding sentence              │
└─────────────────────────────────────────┘
```

図1：Main ideaとsupporting pointsの関係

4-2 Supporting Details

　パラグラフによっては、supporting points をさらに詳説することがあります。その場合、supporting point を示した直後に、具体例や理由を説明する文を続けます。また、引用文や統計、事実などの情報を使うこともあります。いずれも supporting point を補強する働きを担い、**supporting details** と呼ばれます。

　では、実際に次のパラグラフを例に、supporting details がどのように機能しているのか検討してみましょう。

Model Paragraph ②

The Benefits of Working Summer Time Hours in Japan

　　In recent years the introduction of "summer time" working hours has been hotly discussed in Japan. In this model, the conventional working day of 9–5 is shifted so that workers start and finish a couple of hours earlier. This is expected to bring three benefits for companies in Japan. Firstly, it will help them to reduce electricity consumption. Although summer temperatures can be intolerably high during the day, it is relatively cool in the early morning. If workers take advantage of the cooler morning hours, this will mean air-conditioning is used less. Summer time hours are also effective in reducing electricity for lighting, because the workers finish work and leave the office before it gets dark. In addition to reduced power consumption, summer time hours can increase workers' productivity. Overtime has long been part of Japanese corporate culture; the topic of notoriously long working hours is frequently brought up in foreign media. It is likely, however, that the introduction of summer time hours will put pressure on companies to increase their workers' productivity and operational efficiency. This is because the expected benefits of summer time hours will be completely lost if workers start earlier but continue to work late. Finally, summer time hours will allow workers to keep their work-life balance. If workers can leave their company in the late afternoon or early evening, they can spend the rest of the day enjoying a variety of activities. For example, they can participate in sporting activities or join a volunteer group in their neighbourhood and thus become more involved in the community. Another option is to attend adult education courses in subjects of personal interest, or they may stay at home and spend some quality time relaxing with their families. In short, the introduction of summer time hours should be highly beneficial for Japanese companies in terms of improved energy-saving, productivity and employees' work-life balance.

　上のパラグラフでは、日本企業における夏時間の導入（"summer time"）がトピックとして扱われています。第1文と第2文で、夏時間をめぐる議論とそれによる変化を紹介し、第3文で筆者の見解（夏時間の導入は3つの点から効果的である）を述べています。そして続く supporting sentences で3つの supporting points を挙げて、main idea を詳述しています。その際、各 supporting point の後に、その具体例や理由をつけ加えながら説明しています。これらがこのパラグラフの supporting details です。
　モデル・パラグラフ（2）の supporting sentences を分解すると、次のような構造が浮かび上がってきます。

```
┌ Supporting point 1 ·················· 電気量の減少
│      ┌ Supporting detail 1 ········ エアコン（具体例）
│      └ Supporting detail 2 ········ 照明（具体例）
│
├ Supporting point 2 ·················· 効果的な生産性
│      └ Supporting detail ··········· 就業時間の変化（理由）
│
└ Supporting point 3 ·················· ワーク・ライフ・バランスの向上
       └ Supporting detail ··········· 余暇の創出と活用（理由）
              ┌ Example 1 ······ スポーツやボランティア活動
              ├ Example 2 ······ 社会人講座
              └ Example 3 ······ 家族との団欒
```

　上の例からも明らかなように、supporting points も、それらをさらに詳しく説明する

supporting details も、topic sentence で述べられた main idea と密接に関連した内容です。つまり、supporting sentences とは、main idea を展開させ、論証するためにあるのです。Supporting points や supporting details が乏しいと、main idea に説得力を持たせることができません。パラグラフの main idea を定める時には、それを読み手に納得させるに足る情報（具体例や統計データなど）があるかを一考しましょう。その一方で、main idea から外れた余分な情報を盛り込まないようにしましょう。パラグラフの構成を考える時、手元にある情報が本当に main idea と関連しているかを見極めることも重要です。

SECTION 5　Concluding Sentence

5-1　Concluding Sentenceの役割

　パラグラフの最後は結論を示す concluding sentence で締めくくります。これは 1 文程度で終えることが一般的です。パラグラフの要旨を読者に確認させるのが目的で、方法としては主に次の 2 つがあります。

★ Topic sentenceを言い換える。

例）モデル・パラグラフ（1）の concluding sentence

　　Although the sense of these words may be learned by speakers of other languages, they are not easily translatable: they may take a sentence or a paragraph or even a whole page to convey. Such words are an invaluable part of the language and culture that produced them.

★ パラグラフ全体を要約する。

例）モデル・パラグラフ（2）の concluding sentence

　　In short, the introduction of summer time hours should be highly beneficial for Japanese companies in terms of improved energy-saving, productivity and employees' work-life balance.

なお concluding sentence の作成時には、次の 2 点に留意しましょう。

★Topic sentenceをそのまま繰り返したり、酷似した表現を使わない。

英語のアカデミック・ライティングでは、不必要な繰り返しは好ましくないとされます。表現を工夫しましょう（Chapter 1 及び Chapter 5 を参照のこと）。

★新しい議論を導入しない。

Concluding sentence はそれまでの内容をまとめる文です。**ここで新しい議論を展開したり、説明や見解を加えたりしてはいけません**。Topic sentence で述べた main idea を言い換えるか、パラグラフの要点をまとめましょう。

> 🔒 **Concluding Sentence のポイント**
> ・Topic sentence を別の言葉で言い換えたり、パラグラフの要旨を伝える。
> ・Topic sentence とまったく同じ表現は用いない。
> ・新しい議論は持ち込まない。

5-2 Concluding Sentenceを導く便利な表現

モデル・パラグラフ（2）では、"In short," と始めることで、読者に本論の展開が終わり、結びの文に入ることを知らせています。パラグラフの最後（論文では結論を示すパラグラフ）では、モデル・パラグラフ（2）のように、終わりを告げるシグナルがよく使われます。語句や表現として次のようなものがあります。

  In conclusion, . . .
  To conclude, . . .
  Therefore, . . .
  Thus, . . .
  In summary, . . .

To sum up, . . .

In short, . . .

Indeed, . . .

It can be concluded that. . . .

It has been demonstrated/shown that. . . .

The above discussion/analysis/report has argued/demonstrated/suggested/shown. . . .

Practice 2

Read the paragraph and answer the questions.

    Anti-piracy advertising campaigns on behalf of movie studios often equate breach of copyright with stealing, but this equivalence is open to question as a matter of both law and morality. As a matter of law, the crime of stealing or theft has been defined by legal systems for thousands of years as the deliberate taking of another person's physical property; whereas copyright infringement is a relatively recent statutory invention that provides remedies to prevent a person using a copyrighted work in a way that contravenes the exclusive rights of the copyright-holder. Courts have consistently refused to hold that copyright infringement constitutes theft. As a matter of morality, theft permanently deprives the owner of the entire value of the thing stolen, which is a real and concrete loss; in contrast, copyright infringement deprives the copyright-holder of control of the copyrighted work, and of any revenues that might have arisen if the infringer had paid for the movie instead of copying it, but it does not prevent anybody else from paying for the movie if they choose to do so. Although both kinds of loss can be serious, they are qualitatively different in nature and will often be different in degree; it thus makes moral sense to distinguish between them. _____

1. Underline the topic sentence of the paragraph.
2. How many supporting points does the paragraph have?
3. Choose the most appropriate concluding sentence:
    (a) Therefore, we can see that both copyright infringement and stealing are

criminal acts, but they are significantly different crimes and should not be equated.

(b) In short, we should neither infringe copyright nor commit crimes.

(c) To sum up, the way anti-piracy advertising campaigns treat breach of copyright as a crime is not defensible as a matter of both law and morality.

SECTION 6 　UnityとCoherence

6-1 　Unity

　これまでにも強調してきたように、**1つのパラグラフでは、1つのトピックに関するmain idea を1つだけ打ち出します。そして、パラグラフ内のすべての文が main idea に論理的につながるものでなければなりません**。例えば、次のパラグラフには明確な main idea を伝える topic sentence と、それに呼応する concluding sentence がありますが、その間の supporting sentences は必ずしも main idea をサポートしているわけではありません。2〜3のパラグラフに分けて書くべき複数のアイディアが混在しています。このため下のようなパラグラフには **unity**（整合性）がないと見なされてしまいます。

Example
Unityを欠いたパラグラフ

　　　Hollywood movie studios have been remaking successful foreign films for many years. One of the first was French director Julien Duvivier's gangster movie *Pépé le Moko* (1937), which was remade as John Cromwell's *Algiers* (1938), and later as a musical in John Berry's *Casbah* (1948). Perhaps the most famous and most imaginative film remake is the John Sturges western *The Magnificent Seven* (1960), ingeniously based on Akira Kurosawa's *The Seven Samurai* (1954), and recasting the *ronin* as lawless cowboys. Yet often a film is remade without any such creativity, retaining the same story in the same genre and only changing the language and substituting familiar actors. In these cases the goal is seldom artistic and more commercial in nature. The 1980s and 1990s saw a wave of remakes of French comedies such as *Trois hommes et un couffin* (1985), remade as *Three Men and a Baby* (1987); *La cage aux folles* (1978), remade as *The Birdcage* (1996); and *Boudu sauvé des eaux* (1932), remade more than fifty years later as *Down and Out in Beverly Hills* (1986), perhaps the longest gap between an original and its remake. Recent years have seen a shift in Hollywood's interest towards horror movies, such as Hideo Nakata's *Ring* (1998), *Ring 2* (1999) and *Dark Water* (2002), and Swedish director Tomas Alfredson's *Let the Right One In* (2008). It seems certain that Hollywood will continue to mine successful foreign films for fresh material to adapt.

　Unity はパラグラフの必須条件です。パラグラフに unity を持たせるために、複数のトピックが盛り込まれていないか、またすべての文が main idea とつながっているかを必ず検討しましょう。

6-2　Coherence

　英語の文章では、文から文へと進む時（**transition**）に流れを持たせ、パラグラフ全体にまとまり感のあることが大切とされています。これは **coherence**（結束性）と呼ばれます。各文がどんなに文法的に正確で、豊かな語句を用いて作られていても、文章間に流れがなければ、読者は論理展開を追うことができません。文と文の間につながりを生み出すために効果的かつ重要な2つの方法を紹介します。

a Transitional Signals

　第1のポイントは、文と文、節と節の間に適切な表現を用い、論理的な流れを読み手に明示することです。この役割を果たす表現を **transitional signals** と呼びます。Transitional signals にはいろいろな種類があり、逆説や結果、例示など、論理の方向性を示すのに用いられます。その役割を確認するために、最初に transitional signals のないパラグラフを読んでみましょう。

> **Example**
>
> ## Transitional Signalsを欠いたパラグラフ

  A rising exchange rate is often assumed to be a good thing, but the situation is rarely so simple. A strengthening currency often indicates a strong domestic economy, with relatively low unemployment, rising rates of production and an increasing gross domestic product. It suggests confidence in the fundamental strength of the economy and its future prospects for continuing growth. It benefits consumers and companies who import goods and services or make new investments overseas. It benefits overseas travellers. A strengthening currency can also have negative results. It can have a damaging effect on export industries. Exported goods and services become more expensive. Customers prefer to purchase cheaper alternatives from other countries. International tourists will find travel to the country more expensive. They will travel to other places instead. Tourism will suffer. These changes can be very disruptive to the domestic economy. They may give the impression that the economy is out of control. Confidence and investment in the economy may decrease. The currency may fall again. Whether a rise in the exchange rate is positive or negative overall will depend on the circumstances and the makeup of the economy.

 上のパラグラフは正確な文法や語法で書かれており、文単位では問題はありません。しかし、文と文をつなぐ表現が全くないため、文章に流れがありません。このためパラグラフの論理展開をとらえることがきわめて困難です。

 次に示すのは、上のパラグラフに transitional signals（太字）を補ったものです。文と文、節と節の論理的な展開が明確になったため、先ほどの例とは格段の差で理解しやすく、文章全体にまとまりが生まれています。

> **Example**

Transitional Signalsが補われたパラグラフ

　　A rising exchange rate is often assumed to be a good thing, but the situation is rarely so simple. **On the positive side**, a strengthening currency often indicates a strong domestic economy, with relatively low unemployment, rising rates of production and an increasing gross domestic product. **Furthermore**, it suggests confidence in the fundamental strength of the economy and its future prospects for continuing growth. **In addition**, it benefits consumers and companies who import goods and services or make new investments overseas. **Lastly**, it benefits overseas travellers. **However**, a strengthening currency can also have negative results. **For example**, it can have a damaging effect on export industries. **This is because** exported goods and services become more expensive, **so** customers prefer to purchase cheaper alternatives from other countries. **Similarly**, international tourists will find travel to the country more expensive, **so** they will travel to other places instead, **with the result that** tourism will suffer. These changes can be very disruptive to the domestic economy. **Further**, they may give the impression that the economy is out of control. **Consequently**, confidence and investment in the economy may decrease **and** the currency may fall again. Whether a rise in the exchange rate is positive or negative overall will depend on the circumstances and the makeup of the economy.

　文や節をつなぐための表現を機能別に大別すると、追加、対比、選択、類似、原因、結果、例示、順序、言い換えなどの種類が挙げられます。Section 5で学んだconcluding sentenceを導く表現もこの一種です。便利なtransitional signalsとして、次ページのようなものがあります。

便利なTransitional Signals

機能	副詞	副詞句	等位接続詞	従属接続詞	その他
追加・補足をする	moreover furthermore besides also	in addition	and		another＋名詞 an additional＋名詞
反対の意見や、対比・対照を示す	however nevertheless nonetheless	by contrast	but yet	although though while whereas	despite＋名詞（句）
選択・代替案や条件を示す	otherwise alternatively		or	if unless	
類似したことについて述べる	similarly likewise				
原因を示す				because since	
結果を示す	therefore consequently hence thus accordingly	as a result as a conse-quence	so		
例示する		for example for instance			
順序を追って示す	first second third next last finally				the first / second / third ＋名詞 the next / last / final＋名詞
言い換える	namely	in other words that is in fact			

　このようなtransitional signalsを効果的に使うことによって、前ページでみたような流れのある文章を作成できます。ただし使うtransitional signalsの意味や、それが副詞句なのか接続詞なのかを理解したうえで使いましょう。特に、howeverを接続詞として用いたり、andやbutで文を始めることは、アカデミック・ライティングにおいては適切でな

いとされています。不安のある場合は、必ず最初に辞書を引いて例文等で用法を確認しましょう。

またこれ以外にも、前文の内容や議論を受けた表現を使うことで、文と文に論理関係を持たせる方法もあります。これについては Chapter 6 の Section 2 を参照してください。

b 適切な名詞、代名詞の使用

同一文章内で同じ対象を指す名詞や代名詞は、必ず一致させなくてはなりません。特に使われている代名詞に一貫性がないと、その代名詞が何を指しているのか曖昧になります。

次の文章は、「菜食主義者になるには様々な理由がある」という topic sentence で始まり、"People" がその主語に使われています。しかし、続く文章では異なる複数の表現で言い換えられてしまっているため、論の展開を押さえることが困難です。登場する代名詞や名詞に注目しながら読んでみましょう。

　　People may become vegetarian for many different reasons. You might believe that a vegetarian diet is healthier than a diet that involves meat and animal products, and can reduce the risk of certain diseases such as diabetes, heart disease and some forms of cancer. A vegetarian also objects to intensive modern production practices such as factory farming that may cause discomfort, distress or even pain to animals, which can lead to arguments about the kinds of sensations and even emotions felt by non-human animals. You may consider it morally wrong to kill or exploit an animal for food even if it is done humanely, using philosophical arguments similar to those that were once applied to subjects such as slavery. One may also avoid meat for environmental reasons: not only do factory farming practices and intensive fishing produce a significant amount of effluent pollution that can threaten local ecosystems and species, but it has been calculated that the amount of water needed to grow the feed required to produce livestock is many times more than that needed to grow an equivalent amount of protein for direct human consumption. Vegetarianism may often be chosen for more than one of these reasons.

上の文章を、適切な名詞、代名詞を使って書き換えると次ページのような文章になります。

> **Example**
>
> 適切な名詞、代名詞が使われたパラグラフ

People may become vegetarian for many different reasons. **Some vegetarians** believe that a vegetarian diet is healthier than a diet that involves meat and animal products, and can reduce the risk of certain diseases such as diabetes, heart disease and some forms of cancer. **Vegetarians** also object to intensive modern production practices such as factory farming that may cause discomfort, distress or even pain to animals, which can lead to arguments about the kinds of sensations and even emotions felt by non-human animals. **They** may consider it morally wrong to kill or exploit an animal for food even if it is done humanely, using philosophical arguments similar to those that were once applied to subjects such as slavery. **Vegetarians** may also avoid meat for environmental reasons: not only do factory-farming practices and intensive fishing produce a significant amount of effluent pollution that can threaten local ecosystems and species, but it has been calculated that the amount of water needed to grow the feed required to produce livestock is many times more than that needed to grow an equivalent amount of protein for direct human consumption. **They** will often choose vegetarianism for more than one of these reasons.

このように適切な名詞・代名詞を選び、かつ主語や目的語を一貫させることは、coherence のある文章作成のために不可欠です。ことにトピックを指す名詞・代名詞に関してはこのことが重要です。キーワードとなる言葉を定めたら、その人称と数を同一文章の中で常に一致させるようにしましょう。

Section 7 | **Review Exercises**

1. Choose the best example of a paragraph and explain why the others are not good enough.

    (a)   Every comic-book superhero must have a special power. This special power may be acquired from alien physiology or genetic mutation, through an experiment gone wrong, or even through dedicated effort and the application of technology. It may include the ability to fly, superhuman strength, invisibility, the ability to transform one's body at will, or all of the above. Superheroes must also adopt a secret identity. This often involves a costume or other disguise, usually but not always accompanied by a mask, and a professional name such as Superman or Wonder Woman to distinguish the hero from the ordinary person he or she is supposed to be—and may continue to be at times when no crimes are being committed and no super heroic intervention is required. Most superheroes have an arch-enemy, often an evil scientist or master criminal whose fate seems inextricably woven with the hero's, and who often represents the dark side of the superhero's psychology, and a warning always to use special powers for good instead of evil. Superheroes often suffer from psychological trauma owing to some painful event in their past, often involving a close friend or relative, and all tied up in an "origin story" that explains how and why they came to be the way they are today.

    (b)   The main ingredients involved in brewing beer are water, barley, yeast and hops. The brewing process involves many stages, such as malting, mashing, boiling, fermenting, conditioning and filtering. The kind of yeast used in the fermentation process determines whether a beer is classified as an ale or a lager. The most popular beers in the world are lagers, which are top-fermented and often pale and clear; though many producers of ale are cultivating a boutique appeal in parts of the world such as England with their bottom-fermented and darker brews. The World Health Organisation has estimated that as many as 4% of worldwide deaths across sixty types of disease and injury are caused by alcohol. Russia has the world's highest rate of death caused by harmful drinking—as high as 20%. However, experiments in the prohibition of alcohol have often failed spectacularly. For example, the 18th Amendment to the United States Constitution, passed in 1920, was widely blamed for a significant rise in organised crime that often approached outright gang warfare, and it was repealed in 1933. By contrast, smoking has been progressively banned from public places in many jurisdictions, though it is not clear whether it will ever be banned in private.

(c) The modern English language owes much of its richness and variety to the many conquests and invasions that took place throughout the history of the British Isles. The language has its roots in the Anglo-Saxon dialects spoken by the Germanic tribes who invaded Britain in the fifth and sixth centuries. As a result, the most common words in modern English are still words of Germanic origin like *me*, *you*, *man*, *woman*, *mother*, *father*, *day*, *night*, and all the numbers less than a million. Next, the Viking invasions of the eighth to tenth centuries brought a number of Old Norse words to the language, such as *they*, *them*, *anger*, *gift*, *sister* and *skull*. However, the greatest addition to the vocabulary took place following the Norman conquest of 1066, when a vast number of French and Old Norman words passed from the new aristocracy into common speech, including *royal*, *castle*, *courage*, *honour* and *court*. Not infrequently two or more words with the same meaning from different source languages came to co-exist, but subtle differences developed to distinguish them. For example, Anglo-Saxon *sheep* and French *mutton* once meant the same thing, but *sheep* has come to mean a living animal and *mutton* its meat. Without these overlapping influences, English vocabulary would not have become as extensive—and demanding—as it is today.

2. Consider the structure of the following paragraph and put the most appropriate

sentence in each section.

Topic sentence	
Supporting point 1	
Supporting detail 1	
Supporting detail 2	
Supporting point 2	
Supporting detail	
Supporting point 3	
Supporting detail	
Concluding sentence	

a) The identity of the Fair Youth has been debated for centuries, but the question has never been settled.

b) The famous sonnet beginning "My mistress' eyes are nothing like the sun" (Sonnet 130) belongs firmly in this group.

c) The third character is identified as the Rival Poet, who appears in Sonnets 78 to 86.

d) In these sonnets, the poet expresses a deep devotion to the young man in words and phrases that approach and even embrace the language of romantic love, with lyrical lines such as "Shall I compare thee to a summer's day?" (Sonnet 18) and "How like a winter hath my absence been | From thee" (Sonnet 97).

e) Together, these three characters interact in fascinating ways to enrich the entire sequence of Shakespeare's sonnets.

f) The first is the Fair Youth, to whom the first 126 of the 154 sonnets are addressed.

g) Similarly, the Dark Lady of the second major sequence, sonnets 127 to 152, remains a mystery. These sonnets are more passionate and physical than the first group, suggesting an attachment that is explicitly sexual as well as emotional.

h) There are three main characters that can be identified in William Shakespeare's sonnets.

i) The Rival Poet competes with Shakespeare both for the love and attention of the Fair Youth, and for poetic achievement and artistic recognition.

3. Give unity to each paragraph by adding transitional signals, rewriting the text where necessary.

(a) The Hippocratic theory of bodily humours held that all diseases, disabilities and even temperaments resulted from an imbalance in the four basic substances present in the human body: black bile, yellow bile, phlegm and blood. Black bile was thought to originate in the spleen. An excess of black bile would cause a person to become *melancholic*: that is, sad, withdrawn and even despondent. Many poets were thought to be melancholic. Yellow bile was produced by the gall bladder, and too much of it would make a person *choleric*, or angry, irritable and passionate. Military leaders and politicians were often described as choleric. Phlegm came from the lungs. A surfeit of phlegm made a person *phlegmatic*, or passive, lethargic, and calm; a good administrator or civil servant might be thought of as phlegmatic. Blood was produced in the liver but flowed through the arteries and veins. An excess of blood made a person *sanguine*: hopeful, courageous, and optimistic. A very sociable person with many friends, a perfect host or hostess, would be considered sanguine. By considering the proportions of these four humours in the body, physicians from ancient Greece to medieval England could diagnose every condition of the body and the mind.

(b) Many lecturers in the UK feel that motivating their students is a bigger challenge today than decades ago. Most of the reasons are related to the change from an elitist to a mass higher education system. In the 1950s, only a small minority of the UK population participated in higher education, and they tended to stem from a relatively small, homogenous group. The background of students has become increasingly diverse with the rise in participation. Non-traditional students often feel excluded from institutions that are still dominantly white and middle-class, and this sense of exclusion could result in their lower motivation. The expansion of higher education has not led to a proportional increase in funding and facilities. The student-lecturer ratio is higher than it was a generation ago. Students might feel they are treated as anonymous entities and become discouraged. Motivating students from various backgrounds is now a major challenge facing the higher education system in the UK.

4. The following paragraph lacks unity because of topic inconsistency. Change nouns/pronouns and rewrite the text accordingly to keep the argument focused and easy to follow.

Although video games are often seen as a distracting waste of time, they have important benefits that are only now being realised. Single-player video games can provide a sense of purpose, direction and optimism that extends into problems encountered in the real world. One can also enhance one's concentration, reaction time, spatial awareness and hand-eye coordination. A multiplayer game can promote cooperation and communication towards achieving a common goal, whether it be defending the world against aliens or working together in an office. You can learn general problem-solving techniques and even specific physical skills that may be useful in your life or career; in fact, they are used extensively in military training and in professions from aviation to medicine. A video game can teach you to play the guitar, to drive a car or to play tennis better in the real world. Video games have also been developed to help solve difficult problems such as protein folding and effective financing in developing nations. To be sure, a video game can be distracting and can even lead to physical and mental health problems if played to excess. Yet far from being worthless, it has many general and specific advantages that should not be overlooked.

5. Write a paragraph entitled "Benefits of a School Uniform."

CHAPTER 3

エッセイの構造（1）

Section 1 エッセイの3大要素

　Chapter 2 で、パラグラフの基本構造は、「1つの main idea ＋ supporting points」であることを学習しました。学術論文では、このパラグラフの構造を基本として、複数のパラグラフを積み上げることで論の構築を行います。パラグラフの総数は、扱うトピックの大きさや、指定された論文の長さによって異なります。しかし、全体がどれほどの長さであっても、パラグラフの基本と同じく、**1つの論文が扱うトピックとそれについての結論は1つです**。

　英語論文は大別すると、introduction、body、conclusion の3要素から構成されています。エッセイのように比較的短いものは、各要素がパラグラフを基本単位としていますが、学位論文や学術書のように大部になると、それぞれが章単位になります。

　それではエッセイにおいて、3つの要素はどのような働きを持つのでしょうか。具体的な作成法については Chapter 6 で学ぶとして、ここでは各構成要素のポイントを押さえましょう。

★ Introduction
　最初のパラグラフは **introduction**（あるいは introductory paragraph）と呼ばれ、論文で扱う対象（トピック）や、その背景となる情報を示します。そのうえで、トピックについて書き手が最終的に学問的な見地から明らかにすること、すなわち論文の結論（thesis）を提示します。これはパラグラフの topic sentence に該当し、**thesis statement** と呼ばれています。一般的に topic sentence がパラグラフの最初に位置しているのに比して、thesis statement は introduction の最後の方に位置します。

★ Body Paragraphs（Body）
　パラグラフでは、書き手の main idea を supporting sentences で具体的に説明していきました。同じようにエッセイでは、thesis statement を論証するための supporting points を、複数のパラグラフを用いて示します。これらのパラグラフは **body paragraphs** と呼ばれ、本論に当ります。また body paragraphs すべてを指して **body** とも呼びます。Body の各パラグラフも、パラグラフの基本構造「**main idea ＋ supporting points**」で構成されて

います。

★Conclusion

パラグラフの concluding sentence に当たるのが **conclusion**（あるいは concluding paragraph）です。Introduction の thesis statement で提示したエッセイの結論を別の表現で述べたり、body paragraphs の要約を示します。

> 🔒 **エッセイの構造のポイント**
> ・Introduction でエッセイの主張（thesis statement）を示す。
> ・続く body paragraphs において、その主張がなぜ成立し得るかを示す論拠を複数提示する。
> ・Conclusion で再び全体の論の展開と主張を確認する。

SECTION 2　パラグラフとエッセイの関係

　前述したように、エッセイでは「introduction ＋ body ＋ conclusion」という構造をとり、thesis statement でエッセイの主張を先に述べてから、「なぜなら ～」と続けます。パラグラフ内の文すべてが main idea とリンクするように、エッセイでも thesis statement を軸として論を展開させます。パラグラフの基本構造「main idea ＋ supporting points / topic sentence ＋ supporting sentences ＋ concluding sentence」と、エッセイ全体の構造「thesis statement ＋ supporting points / introduction ＋ body paragraphs ＋ conclusion」という展開が呼応しているといえます。

　右の図は、例として 3 つの supporting points を含む、パラグラフとエッセイの構造を示しています。この図が示すように、エッセイは、パラグラフの基本形が複数積み上げられることによって成立しています。また body を構成する各パラグラフも、単独で完結するパラグラフの場合と同じ構造をしており、入れ子細工のような関係になっています。

```
┌─ パラグラフ ─────────────────┐    ┌─ エッセイ ──────────┐
│  Topic sentence (main idea)  │    │  Introduction        │
│  Supporting point 1          │    │  Thesis statement (thesis) │
│  Supporting point 2          │    │  Body paragraph 1    │
│  Supporting point 3          │    │  Body paragraph 2    │
│  Concluding sentence         │    │  Body paragraph 3    │
└──────────────────────────────┘    │  Conclusion          │
                                    └──────────────────────┘
```

図2：パラグラフとエッセイの構造的な関係

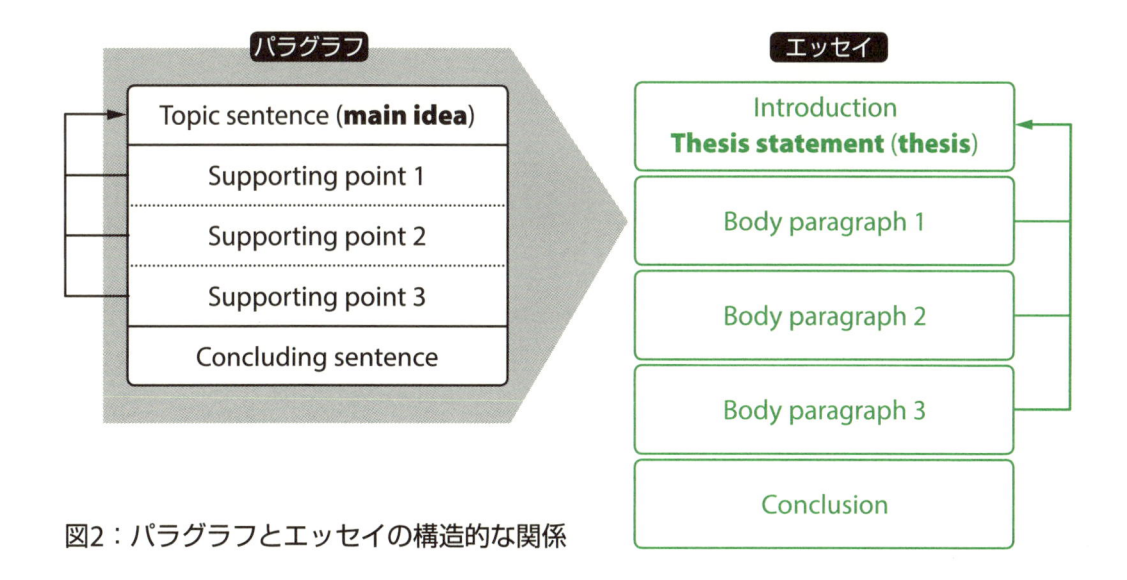

SECTION 3　エッセイのUnityとCoherence

　エッセイ全体で論じられることは、すべてトピックと関連していなくてはなりません。前述したように、bodyの各パラグラフは、thesis statementをサポートする論点を示す役割を担います。またconclusionもbody paragraphsにおける論の展開を踏まえ、エッセイの結論を述べます。すなわちパラグラフと同様、エッセイにもunity（整合性）が欠かせません。Thesis statementを軸にエッセイが論理的に展開するように、しっかりした構成を組み立てることが大切です。

　また、論理的な流れ（**coherence**）があることも重要なポイントです。パラグラフの解説でみたように、文から文、パラグラフからパラグラフへとスムーズな流れのある文章作成を心がけましょう（具体例についてはChapter 6のSection 2を参照のこと）。

SECTION 4　モデル・エッセイを読もう

　このChapterで学んだエッセイの構造について、実例で確認していきましょう。次の点を考えながら、モデル・エッセイを読みましょう。

- エッセイのトピックとthesis statement
- Introduction、body paragraphs、conclusionの位置
- Unityとcoherenceの保ち方（例：どのようにtransitional signalsを使っているか）

Model Essay

エッセイのタイトル

Recognising the Many Dimensions of Academic Writing

Introduction:
トピックに関する情報や背景、先行研究を述べた後、thesis statementを示します。

It is often assumed that academic writing is a primarily mechanical skill that students should be able to apply in any given context. For students who do not possess this ability, remedial classes should be offered to teach them how to write in proper sentences and use correct spelling and punctuation. In the UK separate study skills classes were usually offered to groups considered to be in particular need of such support: international and mature students as well as students from working-class families (Ganobcsik-Williams 3). This approach is still supported by many in the higher education system, but research in linguistics and academic writing has demonstrated that it is too simplistic. For instance the concepts of "academic literacies" and "socioliteracy"—proposed respectively by Lea and Street, and Johns—highlight something necessarily more complex than a formal/technical practice. This essay argues that learning to write academically is indeed more complex than simply mastering the right vocabulary and the rules of syntax, spelling and punctuation.

Thesis statement: エッセイの結論

Body:
Thesis statementを具体的に説明、論証していきます。

The most important reason why writing in any context cannot follow rigid rules in a mechanistic way is the nature of language. Unlike the systems of communication used by animals, human language is not a finite set of expressions that babies learn and repeat. Instead it is a productive system, i.e. a system that allows speakers to say and understand "brand-new combinations of words, appearing for the first time in the history of the universe" (Pinker 22). In order to

引用した文献の著者名とページ数を示します。

communicate via this system, speakers and writers have to be familiar with the rules that govern the use of a specific language. More than that, they have to be able to use them correctly in a specific context. This means that they cannot use a word or grammatical form in a single way whatever the context; instead they need to modulate their use in a way that is appropriate for the meaning they want to convey. Even if there are very stable rules for spelling, for instance, other aspects of language, such as the use of prepositions, vary greatly depending on the meaning a writer wants to express. For example, the verb "report" is not always followed by "to" (e.g. The employee had to report "to" his boss); the right preposition here could also be "on" (e.g. The employee had to report "on" his boss), depending on the context. The need to manipulate language flexibly to express the desired meaning is a crucial characteristic of human language that applies to all its uses, including academic writing.

Another reason why acquiring simple rules about spelling, grammar and vocabulary is not sufficient to become a successful academic writer is the fact that meaning does not exist in a vacuum. It is produced and received in specific situations and those who write and read take on specific roles (Johns 26). The importance of this social context can be easily observed in everyday situations: a student will speak one way to a university lecturer and another way to his or her friends, even if the topic is the same. Similarly, academic writing is shaped by the social context in which it takes place. Such texts reflect the norms of different academic fields in their structure and choice of vocabulary and grammatical forms.

In the English-speaking world the essay is a good example of the way in which text forms are influenced by the shared values of Anglo-Saxon academics. Good essays concentrate on a clearly defined topic that is introduced at the beginning. The argument is then developed through various paragraphs in the main body, before the logical conclusion is presented at the end. The overall structure, or macrostructure, of essays is thus clearly indebted to the Western philosophical tradition, which values linearity and a clear focus on a single topic more than lateral and associative thinking. The need to link paragraphs in a logical way also echoes Western traditions of thought (see, for example, Hutcheon 87). Although students can be taught to write an essay around a single topic, progressing from introduction and body to conclusion, it is more likely that they will succeed in this task if they are familiar with the ideas of logic and linearity.

In the same way it is easier for academic writers to choose appropriate vocabulary and grammatical forms if they are aware of the reasons why an academic community uses them. A good example is the use of an impersonal style of writing. Academic texts tend to avoid referring directly to the writer ("I") or the reader ("you") and use many passive forms ("It has been shown" rather than "I have shown"). Many textbooks on academic writing introduce these forms as being essential for all forms of academic writing, but this generalisation overlooks the variation that can be found from one subject area to another. The sciences are still dominated by the empiricist ideal of objectivity and, therefore, avoid almost any reference to individual persons (Lyotard). Postmodernist approaches in the humanities, on the other hand, argue that subjectivity is unavoidable; as a result, personal forms, such as I, are more often used in this field. The challenge for students is thus not only to learn how to write in an impersonal style, but also to explore how this is used in their specific field of study and why.

In addition to the values of an academic community, texts also reflect the social roles of writers and readers. Although these roles are rarely taught, understanding them is essential for academic writers in order to meet their readers' expectations. As with the use of impersonal forms, the social roles of writers and readers can vary from subject to subject, but also from culture to culture. This gives rise to a common problem for academic writers new to higher education in English-speaking countries. In some cultures respect for one's elders and their greater knowledge means that young academic writers are not allowed to engage critically with their sources and their lecturers' views; in contrast, lecturers in the English-speaking world expect their students to take a critical stance. They have to observe unwritten rules of politeness in their texts, but even relatively inexperienced academic writers can express criticism as long as it is supported by evidence. Discovering one's role as a writer or as a reader in different contexts is, therefore, another important aspect of learning to write academically.

In conclusion, the above discussion has demonstrated the impact of the social context on academic writing. The social roles and values of a community affect the practices of writing and, as a consequence, students cannot become successful academic writers unless they are aware of this context and know how to manipulate language to convey their intended meaning. This means that academic writing should not be considered as a separate, mechanistic skill that can be reduced to formal features, such as correct spelling or punctuation. Nonetheless, the teaching of rules to produce formally correct sentences is still dominant in higher education. This situation urgently calls for a new approach to academic writing, one that embraces its social dimension and truly helps students to become successful academic writers.

Conclusion: Introductionで述べたthesis statementを言い換え、bodyの要点をまとめます。

Works Cited

Ganobcsik-Williams, Lisa. "Introduction." *Teaching Academic Writing in UK Higher Education: Theories, Practices and Models*. Ed. Lisa Ganobcsik-Williams. Basingstoke: Palgrave, 2006. 3-5. Print.

Hutcheon, Linda. *A Poetics of Postmodernism: History, Theory, Fiction*. London: Routledge, 1988. Print.

Johns, Ann M. *Text, Role and Context: Developing Academic Literacies*. Cambridge: Cambridge UP, 1997. Print.

Lea, Mary, and Brian Street. "Student Writing in Higher Education: An Academic Literacies Approach." *Studies in Higher Education* 23.2 (1998): 157-72. Print.

Lyotard, Jean-François. *The Postmodern Condition: A Report on Knowledge*. Trans. Geoff Bennington and Brian Massumi. Minneapolis: U of Minnesota P, 1984. Print.

Pinker, Steven. *The Language Instinct: The New Science of Language and Mind*. London: Allen Lane, 1994. Print.

本文中で引用・言及した文献一覧。著者名等のアルファベット順で並べます。

PART **2**

エッセイを書こう

エッセイ作成と調べるプロセス

全体のプロセス	考える＆書く	調べる
トピック選び	・自分は何に関心があるか考える。 ・いくつか候補を絞る。それぞれについて問いの候補も考える。 ・トピックを1つ選ぶ。	・関心のある事柄について調べる。 ・その候補について調べる。
問いの設定	・そのトピックについて、どのような問いが可能か、意義があるかを考える。 ・明確な問いを設定する。 ・仮の答え（論文の主張）を設定する。	・先行研究を調べる。
仮説・主張の検証、論証	・仮の主張に基づき仮のアウトラインを作成する。主張を検証、論証していく。	・論証に必要な資料を読み、分析する。 ・情報を集め、記録・管理する。 ・自分の主張を発展させていく。
エッセイを書く準備をする	・自分の主張と論証の確認。 ・必要ならアウトラインを修正する。	・論文で引用する資料を選び準備しておく。
エッセイを書く	・アウトラインをもとに書き進める。 ・引用する。 ・文献リストを作成する。 ・全体を一度書き上げたら、編集・推敲へ。時間をおいて何度も読み直す。	・必要であれば継続して調べる。

必ずしもこの通り一直線に進むとは限らず、多くの場合、各段階を繰り返し行き来します。

CHAPTER 4

エッセイの枠組みを構想する

Section 1　問いを立てる

　アカデミック・ライティングとは、単に感想や考えを書き連ねるのではなく、自分が立てた学問的な問いに対する答えを、客観的な立場から論じていくものです。このため執筆を始める前に、自分が何についてどのように論ずるのかを明確にし、対象に関する見解の見通しを立てておく必要があります。その第一歩として、自分の知的関心がどこに向かっているのか、まずは自己の引出しの中に、論文のトピックとなり得る題材を見つける作業を行います。これは「研究テーマ」と説明されるものに当たります。論ずる対象（トピック）を定め、それについて学問的な問いを設定することは、論文作成の全工程に関わるきわめて重要な手続きです。

　人文学系の学問では、読書体験や経験に基づく自分の知的関心を出発点として、トピックを見つけることがあります。しかし、単なる個人的な興味や関心のままでは、学問的な問いとはなり得ません。例えば、ある小説を読んでとても感銘を受けたとします。ですが「感激した」と述べただけでは、感想にすぎません。また、たとえ感銘を受けた理由を詳細に述べたとしても、それもまた個人的な読書体験の追従にしかすぎません。

　研究を行うのも、論文を書くのも「私」という主体ですから、学問的な問いを個人の体験から発することは、否定されるべきことではありません。ここで重要なのは、そうした個人的な関心、問いを、次のステップ、すなわちより具体的な設問へと絞り込み、公共的、普遍的な問いへと押し進めることです。例えば、ある作品、あるいは社会的事件から得た印象を、今度は自分という主体から距離を置いて、より広い文脈や先行研究との関係の中で、客観的、分析的にとらえ直すことが必要になります。それには、自分の得た印象を相対化することを可能とする、読書や知識、また次の Section で詳説する「調べる」ことを要します。

　それでは知的関心や好奇心を出発点として、どのように学問的な問いを立てればよいのでしょうか。

　第1に、**1つの研究／論文で扱う問題が1つに定まっているか**、つまり、扱う問題が抽象的すぎず、論文の長さに適した大きさだろうかと自問しましょう。例えば、中世ヨーロッパ文学の愛読者で、毎日のお風呂を楽しみにしている人が、中世における入浴の文化的意義に関心を持ったとします。しかし、「入浴」というだけでは、あまりにも漠然として大

きすぎますし、問いになっていません。学位論文レベルであれば、「アーサー王伝説における入浴シーンには、どのような文化的表象が反映されているのか」といった問いを立てることができます。しかし、これはエッセイで扱うには大きすぎます。自分がどれほどの規模の論文を書くかによって、トピックの絞り込み方は変わってきます。エッセイ1本程度の長さであれば、例えば、アーサー王伝説作品の中から具体的な作品を1つ選び、そこにおける入浴場面を分析対象の中心に据えるぐらいが適当でしょう。

　第2に、**対象へのアプローチ方法**も考えなくてはいけません。上の例で考えるならば、1つの作品における入浴場面を丁寧に集めて、どのようなアプローチから分析するのかを決めます。その作品における入浴場面の持つ象徴的な意味を考えるのか、歴史的考察を加えるのか、あるいはもう1作品持ってきて比較研究を行うのかなど、アプローチの仕方はさまざまです。対象へのアプローチの方法は学問分野によって異なります。これを学問の方法論といいます。一般に、方法論の詳細については各専門課程で学びます。書き手が専門課程より前段階にあるならば、専門的な理解についてさほど心配する必要はありません。何よりも重要なのは、1つアプローチ方法を定めたら、論文全体でそれを一貫して用いることです。この点を念頭に置いて、論文執筆に取り組みましょう。

　第3に、**扱う情報量**も目安となります。課題に適した大きさにトピックを絞り込み、問いを立てることは、情報の量とも密接に関わってきます。あまりにも壮大な問題を設定してしまうと、それだけ読むべき資料や文献も膨大な量になります。逆に限定的すぎると、関連資料の入手が困難で、客観的な論証ができなくなってしまいます。また次のSectionで述べるように、先行研究の有無も大切です。

　上に述べてきたことは、エッセイ作成時だけに直面する問題ではありません。より根本的な「学問とは何か」ということと深く関わってきます。問いを立て、研究を行うこと、そしてその結果を文章（あるいは口頭発表）によってアウトプットするということは何か。これは学問のいろはであり、大学で学ぶ最重要事項の1つです。この理解なくしては、英語、日本語にかかわらず、優れた論文を生みだすことは難しいでしょう。研究とは何か、論文とは何かということについて、より深く知りたい人は、河野哲也『レポート・論文の書き方入門〈第3版〉』（東京：慶應義塾大学出版会、2002年）、及び、このSectionの典拠となっている佐藤望編『アカデミック・スキルズ―大学生のための知的技法入門〈第2版〉』（東京：慶應義塾大学出版会、2012年）の一読をお薦めします。

> **ONE POINT ADVICE** なかなかトピックが思いつかない、あるいは与えられた一般的なトピックから、具体的なものへと絞り込むことが難しいと感じた場合、ブレインストーミングを行うのも一案です。紙を一枚用意して、自分の思いつくままに自由作文する方法や、頭の中に浮かんできたことをリストアップする方法などがあります。
>
> ブレインストーミングの段階では、有益かどうかといった判断はせずに、とにかく頭の中にある情報や思考をたぐり寄せ、紙の上に書き出すようにしましょう。特にリストアップでは、センテンスを作る必要はありません。文法やスペリングといったことも気にすることなく、深く考え込まずに、出てくるままにどんどん書き出していきます。それを眺めていると、自分がどのようなことに関心を持っているのかを、客体化することができます。また、リストアップ式を繰り返すことで、トピックについて自分が持っている知識や情報を可視化させ、把握することができます。そこから自分が関心のあることについて文献を調べ、知識を深めることで、問題設定の入り口へと近づいてゆくことができます（具体例については、巻末の Appendix 2 を参照のこと）。
>
> 日本の大学のアカデミック・ライティングの授業では、指定されたトピックから 1 つ選び、それを自分で絞り込んで論じる課題が課されることがあります（「環境問題」「教養教育」「伝統芸能」「インターネット」の中から 1 つ選び、それについてより具体的なトピックを設定し、1,500 words 程度で論じなさい、など）。このような場合も、ブレインストーミングを行って自分の思考を客体化することで、例えば「インターネット」のようなテーマについて、自分はどのような知識や関心があるのか、また論を展開させることができるのかを明確にすることができるでしょう。

SECTION 2 なぜ「調べる」ことが必要なのか

レポートや論文を書く時には「調べる」ことが必要だと、多くの人が感じています。そ

の結果、図書館でトピックに関連のありそうな本や記事を探して数多く読み、分かったことをひたすら並べてパッチワークのような論文を書いてしまうことがあります。確かにトピックについての知識は増えるかもしれませんが、調べた内容を継ぎ接ぎしただけの論文では、議論に独自性も発展性もない薄っぺらなものになります。このように、形式的な「調べ物」には落とし穴が潜んでいます。つまり、「調べ物」が目的と化してしまう危険性です。

　では、なぜ「調べる」ことが必要なのでしょうか。これまでにも重ねて述べてきたように、論文作成のプロセスを成すのは、問いの設定と探究です。よって論文とは、その問いに対する答え、つまり自分の意見や見解を「主張」として提示し、「論証」を展開する場です。このような論文作成のプロセスにおいて、「調べる」こと、つまり、リサーチをすることは2つの意義を持ちます。1つは、問いの設定に必要な情報を得ること。もう1つは、結論としての自分の「主張」を導き、検証するために必要な情報を得ることです。

　論文の構想を練り、問いを設定する初期の段階において、トピックについて幅広く情報を集めることは、非常に重要な作業です。トピックについて深い理解がなければ、意味のある問いと主張を設定することはできません。また、そのトピックについてすでに行われてきた研究、つまり、「先行研究」も調べる必要があります。先行研究を調べ、自分が設定した問いについてどのような見解が出されているのかを把握していなければ、自分の意見や見解の妥当性を検討したり、その意義を見極めたりすることはできません。ゆえに先行研究の把握は、自らの問いの設定に不可欠なのです。

　さらに、問いに対する答えを模索する段階では、リサーチで得た情報を活用し、自分の議論を構築していきます。同時に、それを立証するための材料も集めます。よって、この段階では、情報を自分の議論と関連づけて評価することが必要になります。もはやトピックそのものについての知識を得る段階ではないので、自分の論文の内容に深く関連した、より専門的な内容の文献資料に当たることが必要になってきます。この際、得られた情報や見解が自分が賛成できるものとは限りません。出版された本の著者は専門家と呼ばれる権威のある人物であることが多いので、そこで述べられたことをそっくりそのまま受け入れがちです。しかし、他の人の意見や見解に疑問を持ったり、反対の意見を持ったりすることは、その理由を論理的に説明できる限りは、奨励されるべきことです。本来、アカデミックな世界は「主張の場」であるだけでなく、むしろ「意見が行き交う」開かれた場でもあります。自分と同じ意見、似た意見でありながら着眼点や論理の筋道が違う見解や、全くの反対意見を知ることで、独りよがりに陥らず、自分の見解の妥当性を複数の視点から吟

味し、問題があればそれに気づくことができるようになります。自分の主張そのものが変わることはなかったとしても、より深みのある吟味された議論を展開することができるのです。

なお、文献の種類や収集に関する詳細は、Chapter 5 で学びます。

SECTION 3　エッセイの骨組みを作成する

3-1　アウトラインとは

　問題設定を行い、文献収集によって問いに対する答えの方向性を見出したら、次に論文全体の見通しを立てます。具体的には、文献の検討に基づき thesis statement を定め、論文の設計図の役割を果たす**アウトライン（outline）**を作成します。

　論文の真髄は thesis statement にあります。しかし、たとえどんなに立派な thesis statement であっても、これを読み手に理解し、納得してもらえなければ意味がありません。それゆえ、論文の基本構造「introduction + body + conclusion」という展開を押さえ、論理的かつ客観的に議論を構築していくことがきわめて重要です。これを論文執筆のうえで実現させるために欠かせない作業が、アウトラインの作成なのです。アウトラインの作成には、次のような目的があります。

> **アウトラインの目的**
>
> ・Thesis statement を定める。
> ・Supporting points をどのような順番で論じるかを整理する。
> ・文献収集で得た情報のうち、何をどこで使うかを整理する。

　最初から完璧なアウトラインを作成できるわけではありませんし、それを目指す必要もありません。むしろ研究や論文執筆が進むにつれて、トピックに関する自分の思考が深まり、それに伴い構成や情報の取捨選択も変わってきます。このため執筆の途中でアウトラ

インの軌道修正が必要になることもあります。例えば本書の作成過程で、微調整も含めると、筆者たちはアウトラインを7回書き換えました。最初に立てたアウトラインに変更を加える場合、少し時間を置き、できるだけ客観的な視点で見直すようにすると良いでしょう。また第三者からのフィードバックも参考になるでしょう。

3-2 アウトラインの作成方法

　論文の構成要素を明確にし、各要素がどのように関係するかをはっきりさせるため、アウトラインを作成する際には、ローマ数字（Ⅰ、Ⅱ、Ⅲ...）やアラビア数字（1、2、3...）、アルファベットなどを使って視覚化させます。アウトラインの作成にはいくつか方法がありますが、ここでは一般的な例を紹介します。

★ Step 1

　最初に論文の3大要素、introduction、body paragraphs、conclusion という大きな枠組みを、ローマ数字を使って作成します。Introduction の項には、thesis statement を、body paragraphs の項にはそれぞれの main idea（topic sentence あるいはその要点）を示します。

　下の例は body paragraph が3つの場合です。ここではローマ数字のⅡ～Ⅳが body paragraphs を構成します。当然のことながら、パラグラフの総数は論証する内容と量によって変わってきます。例えば、1,500 words 程度のエッセイであれば、introduction と conclusion はそれぞれ1パラグラフ、body paragraphs は3～5パラグラフぐらいを目安にすると良いでしょう。

　　Ⅰ. Introduction
　　　　Thesis statement
　　Ⅱ. First main idea
　　Ⅲ. Second main idea
　　Ⅳ. Third main idea
　　Ⅴ. Conclusion

★Step 2

　次に body paragraphs の下位層を考えます。Chapter 2 で学んだように、1 つのパラグラフは、1 つの main idea とそれを説明したり立証する supporting points から構成されます。また各 supporting point を supporting details によって具体的に説明します。Chapter 3 でみたように、各 body paragraph はこの構造を保ちながら、introduction の thesis statement の論拠を示していきます。アウトライン作成時に、それぞれの body paragraph でどのような supporting point を示すのか、それにはどのような情報やデータを使うのかを明確にします。表示の仕方としては、supporting point にはアルファベットを使い、それを補足する supporting detail には数字を使います。

　Ⅰ. Introduction
　　　Thesis statement
　Ⅱ. First main idea (topic sentence)
　　　A. First supporting point
　　　　　1. First detail
　　　　　2. Second detail
　　　B. Second supporting point
　　　　　1. First detail
　　　　　2. Second detail
　　　［後略］

　上記をまとめると、ローマ数字等を用いたアウトラインの基本形は、次のように図示できます。繰り返しになりますが、ここで示す main idea や supporting point/detail の数は例にすぎず、実際の数は、書き手が持っている情報やデータの量によって決定されます。

★アウトラインの基本形
　Ⅰ. Introduction
　　　Thesis statement
　Ⅱ. First main idea (topic sentence)
　　　A. First supporting point

    1. First detail
    2. Second detail
   B. Second supporting point
    1. First detail
    2. Second detail
   C. Third supporting point
    1. First detail
    2. Second detail
    3. Third detail
 Ⅲ. Second main idea (topic sentence)
   A. First supporting point
    1. First detail
    2. Second detail
   B. Second supporting point
    1. First detail
    2. Second detail
 Ⅳ. Third main idea (topic sentence)
   A. Supporting point
    1. First detail
    2. Second detail
 Ⅴ. Conclusion

　このように論文全体の枠組みを最初に作ることで、thesis statement を軸として論を展開させるための道筋をつけることができます。アウトラインの作成によって、論文作成における最大のポイント、「主張 + 論証」という枠組みの基礎固めを行い、論文の方向性を具体的に定めるのです。逆にいうと、知識や情報が何もない段階でアウトラインを作ることはできません。アウトラインの作成を行うのは、文献調査を終えて問いに対する仮説ができた段階です。しっかりとしたアウトラインができれば（それを後で改稿することはあっても）、論文の大筋は整ったといえるでしょう。
　なおアウトラインの実例については、Chapter 6 の Review Exercises と Chapter 7 にあ

るモデル・エッセイを参考にしてください。

3-3 タイトルを考える

　論文のタイトルは、読み手が最初に目にするところです。これから何について述べるのか、どのような結論を導き出すのか、論文のエッセンスを読み手に伝える役目を担います。このため論文のトピックとそれに関する書き手の主張を最もよく表す thesis statement の内容を凝縮させて作成します。

　Chapter 3 で読んだモデル・エッセイのタイトルは "Recognising the Many Dimensions of Academic Writing" でした。このように、一般的に英語論文のタイトルは、完結した文ではなく、名詞形で表します。なかには引用文を用いたり疑問文を使ったりすることがありますが、初学者がこうした手法を取ることはお薦めしません。

　形式的なことにも約束事があります。まずタイトルの最初の文字は大文字にします。そしてタイトル内の名詞、動詞（句）、形容詞などは大文字で始め、より重要度の低い冠詞、前置詞、等位接続詞などは小文字のままにします。またタイトルの後にピリオドは打ちません。ただし副題をつける場合は、コロン（:）を使って結び、コロンの後はスペースを1つ空け、大文字で始めます。

ONE POINT ADVICE　論文の執筆が進むにつれて、最初に選んだトピックに限界を感じ、途中で変えたくなる衝動にかられることがあるかもしれません。どうしても先に進めなくなった場合には、トピックの絞り方や問いの立て方に何らかの問題があると考えられます。その場合は、もう一度原点に戻って見直す必要があります。その一方で、トピックを途中で変更するということは、あらたに多くの時間と労力を要します。限られた時間の中で良質のものを生み出すためにも、これはできるだけ避けたいことです。そのためにも論文執筆に向けた準備段階で熟考を重ね、先の見通しを立てることが肝要です。

CHAPTER 5

文献資料の扱い方

SECTION 1　文献資料について

1-1　どのような文献資料が必要か

　論文で扱われる文献資料は一次資料と二次資料に区別されます。一次資料とは、文学作品、芸術作品、雑誌や新聞、旅行記や日記など、それ自体が研究対象となる資料を指します。二次資料は、一次資料について解説した文書や、研究書や統計資料などを指します。学術分野や論文の内容によって、扱う一次資料と二次資料の割合は変わります。また、研究の内容によっては、同一の資料が一次資料にも二次資料にもなり得ます。例えば、新聞記事は二次資料として扱われることが多いですが、ある特定のトピックに関する記事を数多く集め、そのトピックの扱われ方に歴史的な変遷があることを示す場合、それらの新聞記事は一次資料となります。

　一般的に、論文中の論証に必要になるのは、主に二次資料です。どのような文献資料が有効かは、論文の内容に関わります。社会科学的な内容の論文では、統計データがよく用いられるかもしれません。例えば、日本の大学の奨学金制度拡充を訴える論文では、他国と比較するために、OECDから発表されている、親が学費を負担する割合を国別に調査した結果を持ち出すことが有効かもしれません。しかし、文学作品についての論文では、統計データを使うことはごくまれといえるでしょう。その代り、作品そのものが一次資料として議論の中心になり、二次資料によって、文学批評家・研究家と呼ばれる専門家の見解を提示します。いずれにしろ、自分の論文の議論に必要な資料を見極め、適切な段階で効果的に用いることが重要です。

1-2　収集した情報の評価

　どのような種類の文献資料を用いるにしても、**情報の客観性**と**信頼性**を見極めることが重要です。客観的な論証を行うために外部からの情報を用いているのに、その情報が客観性に欠けるなど、信頼できないものであったら意味がありません。この問題が特に深刻になるのはインターネット上の情報です。インターネットは正しく使えば情報収集の大いなる助けとなります。しかし、そこで得られる情報を取捨選択できなければ、潜在的に多く

の危険を孕んだ情報媒体でもあります。論文執筆時には、主に2つの判断材料が取捨選択の決め手となります。1つは、情報の発信者が特定でき、信頼できること。例えば、匿名で書かれたウェブサイト上の情報は、情報発信者としての責任が問われないため、不正確である可能性があります。また、匿名でない場合でも、実在の人物かどうか、または、その情報を発信するだけの専門的見識を有した人物かどうか、特定することは困難です。情報の取捨選択のもう1つの決め手は、情報の客観性、信頼性が判断可能であることです。例えば、実験やアンケートの場合、実施条件や方法についての詳細な情報が提供されていなければ、その結果が客観的で信頼できるものであるか判断ができません。また、利害関係がある問題の場合、中立的な立場から発信された情報かどうかを見極める必要があります。例えば、思想や活動において過激な自然保護団体が存在するとしましょう。この団体は、環境破壊の被害を訴えるために、その規模を非科学的な方法で大きく見積もったり、反証材料を排除して自らに有利な情報のみを提示している可能性があるかもしれません。大学や研究所など第三者的立場にある機関が提供する情報のほうが客観性が高いといえます。

1-3 論証が必要かどうか

　論証とは、議論の余地のある見解や意見について行うものです。逆にいえば、議論の余地のないもの、つまり、「事実」について論証を行う必要はありません。例えば、「ハワイは太平洋上に位置している」とか「日本の首都は東京である」と述べる際に、わざわざ文献資料を用いて立証する必要はありません。しかしながら、一般に「事実」とされていることでも、学術分野によっては論争の余地があると認識されていることもあります。そのため、何を立証の必要のない「事実」ととらえるかは、慎重に判断せねばなりません。この判断を正確に行うには、文献資料を読みこみ、学術的な見解の動向を把握することが助けとなります。

　同様に、「なんとなく皆そう思っている」こと、「世間一般でよくいわれること」でも、客観的・科学的に真実であることが明らかでない限り、それを前提として議論を構築すべきではありません。例えば、「今の日本の若い人は皆内向きで野心がない」という意見をよく聞きます。しかし、「日本の若い人」とは何歳から何歳を指すのでしょうか。日本に居住する人を指すのか、日本国籍を有する人を指すのかも曖昧です。そのうちの何％が「皆」に該当するのでしょうか。「内向き」かどうか、「野心」のあるなしは何をもって判

断するのでしょうか。そもそも「内向き」の状態とはどのように定義されるのでしょうか。アカデミックな論文において、このような一般的な説を前提に議論を進めてしまうと、説得力のない論文になってしまいます。通説（例えば、文化現象や社会傾向、国民性などに関していわれること）はそのまま受け入れるのではなく、文献資料から科学的・客観的に裏づけられるか慎重に見極めましょう。

1-4 剽窃に注意する

　先に説明したように、文献資料を通して、研究動向を把握し、複数の見解を認識することは自分の見解を確立し、議論を発展させるうえで大変重要です。しかし、論文で文献資料を扱う時は**剽窃**（plagiarism）に該当する行為を行わないよう留意しなくてはなりません。Chapter 1 で説明したように、剽窃は簡単にいうと盗作で、他人の言葉、情報、考え方を、自分のものであるかのように使用することを指します。アカデミックな決まり事を知らないでいると、意図せずに剽窃に該当することをしてしまうことがあります。剽窃を避けるためにはまず、情報が自分のものでないことを、定められた形式（本書では MLA 方式）で明らかにすることが大切です。具体的には、引用や要約の仕方、情報の出典を明示する方法を学ぶ必要があります。これらについては、この Chapter の後半部で詳しく説明します。

SECTION 2　文献資料を集める

　Part 2 の冒頭で「エッセイ作成と調べるプロセス」として示したように、実際の執筆に向けて複数のプロセスを踏まえた文献収集や調査を行います。簡単にまとめると、次のようなステップがあります。

★Step 1
　関心のある事柄について、様々な書物や雑誌記事などに目を通し、トピックの候補を考える。

★Step 2
選んだトピックについて幅広い情報を集め、どのような問題設定が可能かを考える。
★Step 3
絞り込んだトピックに関する情報や先行研究を集める。
★Step 4
論文で引証できる材料を揃える。

　一般的に、Step 1 は日常の読書や授業、新聞・テレビ・インターネットなどを通した情報収集、あるいは自分の体験の中で生まれてくるでしょう。学術論文において特に大切なのは、Step 2 以降です。自分の関心の対象が、学術的な問いとなり得るかを見極め、仮説を立て、論証するための材料を揃えていきます。必要となる具体的な文献収集の方法は、厳密にいうと専門分野によって差異がありますが、ここでは一般的な（学部1・2年時の一般教養課程レベルで必要とされる）文献収集の方法を以下に簡潔にまとめておきます。Step 1 には、a や b が、Step 2 以降には、a、及び c 以降（特に Step 4 には d）が有効でしょう。

a 蔵書検索

　普段から図書館のオンライン・カタログを使っている人は多いでしょう。最近は大学その他の専門図書館だけでなく、公立図書館でもオンライン・カタログが整備され、自宅からも蔵書を検索することができるようになっています。いわゆる「簡易検索」に慣れ親しんでいる人が多いと思いますが、詳細な条件を設定した検索方法など、検索のコツを知っておくと、求めている資料に行き当たりやすくなります。大学図書館では、検索方法の説明会などが開催されていることもあるので、機会があれば是非参加しましょう。

b 書棚をブラウジングする

　図書館でも書店でもいいので、関心のあるトピックについての本が集まっているあたりをぶらりとしていると、オンライン・カタログでは行き当たらなかった文献資料が見つかることは意外と多いものです。また、馴染みのないトピックや分野のセクションを眺めて

いると、新たな興味が見つかったりします。書棚のぶらり散歩は、知的関心を高めるのに非常に効果的です。

c 芋づる式に見つける

　いくらオンライン・カタログや書棚を探しても、これという資料が見つからない場合は、一般に芋づる式と呼ばれる方法に頼ります。まずは限られてはいても入手できた資料を読み、その中で言及されている資料や参考文献リストを利用し、新たな文献や資料を発掘します。逆に、文献が多すぎて絞り込むのが難しい時、先行研究で重要とされている文献が分からない時にも、芋づる式が有効です。いくつか文献を読み、参考文献リストを調べると、引用されている頻度が顕著に高いものが見つかるはずです。そういった文献は、当該分野で重要視されているものだとみなしてよいでしょう。

d 雑誌新聞記事検索を利用する

　専門分野に関する先行研究（特に学術雑誌掲載の研究論文など）を網羅的に調べるには、専門に特化したデータベースを利用するのが一番です。専門分野によって利用するデータベースは異なるので、担当教員に訊いたり、図書館のレファレンスカウンターなどでアドバイスを求めるとよいでしょう。

　またニュース記事を調べたい時にも、データベースが便利です。下に紹介したLexisNexis® *Academic* 以外にも、各社が制作するオンライン版などもあります。

　以下に、人文学全般で代表的なものの一部を紹介します。データベースには、一般公開されているものと、図書館などの機関が有料契約をしていないと使えないものがあります。後者には * をつけています。

★海外
- **JSTOR*** <http://www.jstor.org/>
　人文、社会、経済・経営、科学などの学術雑誌のバックナンバーを電子的に保存する。
- **LexisNexis®** *Academic** <http://www.lexisnexis.com/hottopics/lnacademic/>
　世界各国の主要なニュース（新聞・雑誌・通信社）、法律、企業、人物情報などを収録。

▶ **CSA Illumina*** <http://www.csa.com/>
　CSA (Cambridge Scientific Abstracts) が作成する抄録・書誌データベースを提供するインターフェース。社会科学、図書館情報学、美学、心理学など様々な分野を対象としている。

▶ **EBSCOhost*** <http://search.ebscohost.com/>
　EBSCO Information Services が製作する外国雑誌の全文、抄録・書誌データベースを提供するインターフェース。上に挙げた CSA Illumina と同様、幅広い専門分野のデータベースを個別に検索したり、複数のデータベースを指定して横断検索することができる。

▶ **Google Scholar** <http://scholar.google.co.jp/>
　Google 社が提供する論文サーチエンジン。学術論文や書籍等を分野を問わず検索することが可能。

★ 国内

▶ **CiNii（国立情報学研究所）** <http://ci.nii.ac.jp/>
　学協会刊行物や大学紀要を中心とし、主に国内の学術論文情報を幅広く調べることができる。

▶ **NDL-OPAC(国立国会図書館蔵書検索・申込システム)** <https://ndlopac.ndl.go.jp/>
　国立国会図書館が所蔵する資料 (図書や雑誌・新聞など)、および雑誌記事の検索・申込みができる。

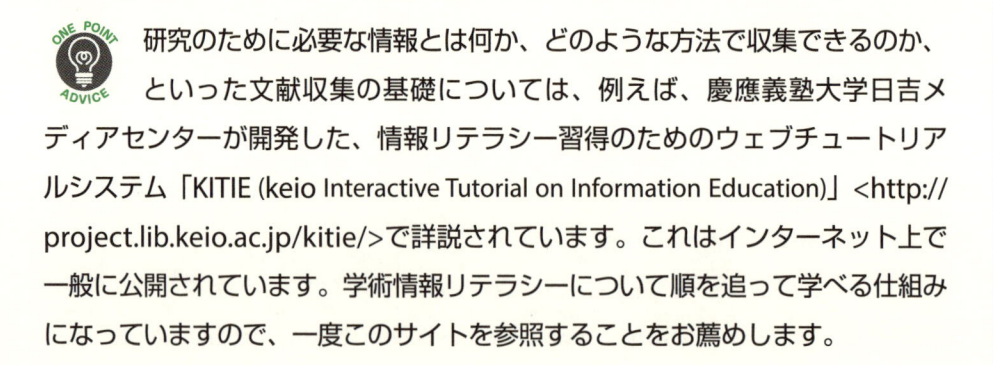

> **ONE POINT ADVICE**　研究のために必要な情報とは何か、どのような方法で収集できるのか、といった文献収集の基礎については、例えば、慶應義塾大学日吉メディアセンターが開発した、情報リテラシー習得のためのウェブチュートリアルシステム「KITIE (keio Interactive Tutorial on Information Education)」<http://project.lib.keio.ac.jp/kitie/>で詳説されています。これはインターネット上で一般に公開されています。学術情報リテラシーについて順を追って学べる仕組みになっていますので、一度このサイトを参照することをお薦めします。

SECTION 3　文献資料の情報管理

3-1　情報管理の目的と意義

　リサーチを進め、数多くの文献資料を扱っているうちに、各文献の内容や書誌情報を記憶しておくことが難しくなってきます。これらの情報を整理し、その記録を管理しておくと、必要な情報がすぐに見つかり、論文執筆が効率的に進みます。

　しかし、文献資料の情報を記録整理する一番の意義は、その作業を通して収集した情報をクリティカルに分析することにあります。Chapter 4 で「調べ物」が目的と化してはいけないと述べましたが、リサーチはあくまでも自分の論文の議論を発展させるために行うものです。よって、文献資料に当たる時には、漫然と読むのではなく、その情報が自分の論文と関連があるかどうかを見極め、関連があるとすればどの点においてかを考えながら、分析的に読むことが大事です。読んだ後には、文献資料の内容を要約し、特に自分の論文に重要な点、その他のコメントを書き留めておきます。また、印象的あるいは独創的な文言があれば、それも記録しておきます。そうすれば、論文執筆時に引用したいと思った時に、すぐに見つけられて便利です。こうして記録を残しておくことで、論証材料として活用できる情報を蓄積していくことができます。そして、自分なりのシステムを確立してこれらを管理しておけば、必要な情報がすぐに見つけられ、実際に論文を書く作業がはかどります。

3-2　情報の記録と管理の方法

　具体的な文献資料の記録や管理の方法は、後から必要な情報がすぐに引き出せるシステムであれば、後は一番自分にあった方法を選べばよいでしょう。例えば、パソコンで記録を作成しておくと検索機能が使えて便利ですが、手書きでメモをするのを好む人もいます。

　記録の取り方には大きく2つあります。1つは、原文の一部を直接抜粋して転記する方法、もう1つは、自分の言葉で置き換えて同じ内容を表現する方法です。後者のタイプである **paraphrase（言い換え）** と **要約** の方法については、次の Section で詳しく説明します。

　記録を取る際は、意図しない剽窃を避けるために2つの点に留意します。第1に、記

録する文言が原文から直接抜粋されたものか、または、自分の要約あるいは言い換えであるか、その区別を明確にしておきます。この区別が曖昧だと、論文で引用する際に文献資料を読み返して確認する必要が生じます。さらに、特定の部分を直接抜粋する場合は、原文に忠実に、正確に転記します。引用符とページ数をつけておけば、それが直接引用されたことが分かりやすくなるでしょう。要約をする場合には、元の文章の構造や表現をそのまま使わないよう、くれぐれも注意しましょう。

　各文献資料の記録の取り方は最終的には自分に合ったものを選ぶとよいと説明しましたが、以下に情報整理の一例を挙げますので参考にしてください（また、本書巻末のAppendixに文献資料の記録ページを収録しています）。

Example

Duncan, Phyllis. *The Fiction of Beryl Pym*. Lewis: Howell P, 2009. Print.

Summary:
The author argues that Beryl Pym is far less traditionalist than she is often believed to be. She creates highly realistic and rounded characters but makes sure that the reader knows that they are fictional characters. She argues that this is not a conventional realist practice.

Quotations:
"Pym's deceptively affective narrative voice successfully conceals the dark side of human psychology from the surface of the story. Nonetheless, it manages to reveal the hidden human psyche at the most crucial moments and shocks the readers" (35).
"Pym is one of the most ingenious and ambitious practitioners of literary conventionalism in post-war British fiction" (89).

Comments:
The author's argument is not fully convincing. Her approach to fiction is too

> straightforward. She often relies on Pym's biographical details and speculates about her authorial intentions. At the same time she overlooks Pym's numerous comments about her attachment to the English realist tradition.

SECTION 4　引用

4-1　引用の意義と種類

　Chapter 4 で説明したように、問いについて自分なりの答えを見出し、論文でそれを論証していく際に、専門家の見解や関連する資料統計を挙げることは、議論に説得力を与えるうえで大変重要です。客観的で科学的な論証材料もないまま、ひたすら自分の意見を説明したのでは、論文ではなく、随筆か感想文になってしまいます。

　しかし、できる限り数多くの文献資料から情報を引用すればよいというわけではありません。引用ばかりが並んだ論文というのは、独創性も説得力も欠ける印象を与えます。引用するかどうかの判断材料として、その情報が論文の議論に深く関連しており、その展開に不可欠かどうかを自問しましょう。引用はあくまでも、自分の議論の論証のためであることを忘れてはいけません。

　さらに、引用をする場合は、引用した情報の関連性や意義が読み手に分かるよう配慮しましょう。特に、いきなり文献資料からの抜粋を挿入し、その内容について何の解説もせず、引用に「語らせる」のは避けるべきです。これは、引用した情報を自分の議論と関連づけ、その意義を説明することをせず、それを読み手が正しく察するだろうと勝手に期待していることに等しい行為です。書き手には引用の意義が明らかであるように思われても、それを丁寧に説明しない限り、読み手には理解できないかもしれません。この説明を怠り、読み手を困惑させるような論文は、「分かりやすく伝える」というアカデミック・ライティングの重要な条件を満たしていないことになります。

> 🔒 **引用のポイント**
> ・論証に絶対不可欠な情報のみ含める（引用はどれだけ調べたか、知っているかを披露する場ではない）。
> ・引用に語らせない！
> ・引用の意義が読み手に明らかであるようにする。

引用の種類には、大きく分けて、直接引用と間接引用の 2 つがあります。どちらの場合も、出典を文末に括弧内で明示します。出典情報の示し方については、この Chapter の Section 5 で説明しています。

4-2　直接引用

直接引用では、元の文章から特定の語や表現をそのまま引用します。ただし、直接引用をするのは、元の文言そのものが価値を持つ場合に限ります。例えば以下のような場合です。
・独創的で印象的な表現である。
・指摘したい問題などを、きわめて的確に表現している。
・その表現を直接引用することが、論文の議論に不可欠である。

> **直接引用の基本**
> ・引用部分が原文であることを示すために、引用部分は二重引用符「" "」でくくる。引用部分内で引用符が使用されている場合は、元の引用符が二重であっても、一重引用符「' '」を使う。
> ・文をまるごと引用する必要はなく、単語や句だけでもよい。
> ・引用を地の文の一部として挿入した時、文全体が文法的に成立するようにする。

> **Example**

According to Peter Williams, "the company made the most successful strategic move in its history by buying out the failing bank" (23).

> **Example**

Murdoch considered his first poem a failure and wrote in a letter to his friend that "'The Venus and the Bubbles' was a colourless and empty invention of the youth" (67).

　4 行以上の長い文章を引用する場合は、地の文から独立させます。地の文の後に 1 行を空け、そこに引用した文章を配置します。引用部分は地の文の左端から半角 5 スペース分内側にインデントします。引用符は不要です。引用部分の句読点の後に括弧を置き、出典情報を示します（短い引用の場合と句読点の処理が異なるので注意。詳しくは Section 5 を参照のこと）。

> **Example**

The use of the word "English," which automatically leaves out people in Wales, Scotland and Northern Ireland, has always been controversial. The word "British" therefore has been considered to be a safe option. This designation, however, is not without contention:

> In recent years, partly as a response to the devolution of political power to Scotland, Wales and Ireland, there has been much questioning of what it means to be British. If we are all British, then why should people feel a need to revert to their previous "nationalities"? And if others in the UK have power devolved to them, what becomes of the formerly dominant English? (Storry and Childs 3-4)

Such national sensitivity, shaken by devolution and vanishing "Englishness," made acceptable the politically charged rhetoric concerning "British value," which plagued the last general election.

そのまま引用すると意味が不明確な場合は、原文に情報を補足します。ただし、オリジナルの部分と区別できるように、追加情報は［ ］に入れます。

Example

Westwood remarks in his essay that "the experience was incredibly inspirational," so much so that he produced his first collection of poems in three months (35).

▶▶ Westwood remarks in his essay that "the experience [of meeting his mother for the first time] was incredibly inspirational," so much so that he produced his first collection of poems in three months (35).

Example

In her diary Kate wrote, "He will be a successful writer" (Middleton 41).

▶▶ In her diary Kate wrote, "He [her younger brother] will be a successful writer" (Middleton 41).

また、比較的長い文章を引用する場合、一部を省略することが可能です。ただし、文法的に整合性がある形で省略し、省略箇所には「. . .」を挿入します。「. . .」の前後にはスペースを1つ空けます。省略箇所の場所によって句読点の処理などが必要になることがありますので、詳しくは *MLA Handbook* で確認してください。

Example

"The invention of affordable cars for families, although one of the earliest models cost almost half the average annual family income, drastically changed how people organised their daily life" (Grant 28).

▶▶ "The invention of affordable cars for families . . . drastically changed how people organised their daily life" (Grant 28).

4-3 間接引用

間接引用では、paraphrase や要約によって、元の文章の言葉を使わずに、その内容を

伝えます。

a Paraphrase

Paraphrase とは、文章を自分の言葉で書き換え、元の文章の内容を伝えることです。*Oxford Advanced Learner's Dictionary* (7th ed.) では、"to express what somebody has said or written using different words, especially in order to make it easier to understand" と説明されています。

Paraphrase で重要なのは、原文の意味を正確に理解し、それを自分の言葉で忠実に表現することです。しかし、表現力や語彙力が限られている時に、いきなり自分の言葉で表現するのはとても難しいことです。慣れないうちは、重要な単語を1つずつ、同義語と置き換えるところから始めてもよいでしょう。ただし、単語を置き換えただけでは十分な paraphrase とはいえず、それを論文中で用いた場合、剽窃になってしまいます。剽窃を避けるためには、原文の形跡を残さない程度の、句や文単位での言い換えが必要です。

Paraphrase には、類義語辞典が大変役に立ちます。ただし、Chapter 1 で説明したように、単語の定義を見る限り同じ意味を持っているように見えても、微妙な意味の違いがあり、同じ文脈で使えない場合があります。必ず英英辞典で意味と語法を最終確認して、元の文章の意味を正確に伝えられるようにしましょう。

🔒 Paraphrase のポイント

・対象の文章の意味を把握する。
・その意味を変えないように注意しながら、自分の言葉で表現する。元の文章の構造や表現をそのまま使わないように注意する。

Example & Practice

次ページの (1) はあるパラグラフの冒頭です。(2) と (3) はそれを paraphrase したものですが、どちらも問題があります。何が問題なのでしょうか。

(1) One of the factors which affect the nature and quality of learning is whether motivation comes intrinsically or extrinsically. This distinction in the origin of motivation is based on the perception that the factors underlying motivation can be located either inside or outside a person. Thus, someone who is intrinsically motivated to learn about an academic subject is driven by his or her own interest in this subject and the sense that the learning experience in itself is enjoyable (Power 59-60).

(2) One of the factors which influence the nature and quality of learning is whether motivation comes internally or externally. This idea is based on the concept that what underlies motivation can be found either inside or outside a person. So a person who is internally motivated to learn academically is inspired by his or her own interest in this subject and the awareness that the learning experience itself is fun (Power 59-60).

(3) Where one's motivation comes from determines one's learning experience. The distinction between intrinsic and extrinsic motivation is founded on the idea that it comes either from within or outside oneself. A person with intrinsic motivation is driven to learn not by her or his love of the subject but by the anticipation of the reward that learning the subject would bring, such as a good career.

　(2) は文法的には正確な文章が続いていますが、言い換えがされたのは単語くらいで、文構造はほぼ変わっていません。(1) と並置してみると、ほぼ全体が (1) のコピーであるのが分かります。このレベルの paraphrase は剽窃に該当します。
　(3) は単語だけでなく、文構造も大幅に変わっています。言い換えの余地が限られているキーワード（例えば、intrinsic/extrinsic/motivation）は使われていますが、他は (1) の元の文の形跡がほとんどありません。ですが、この paraphrase は正確さに問題があり

ます。というのも、最後の文では、元の文の意味と全く逆の内容のことを述べているからです。

さらに、原文にあった出典情報が（3）では省略されています。これはささいな点に思えるかもしれませんが、看過できません。情報源を明示しなければ、それを自分の意見や見解として提示していることになり、盗用に該当します。先に指摘したように、論文作成における決まり事を理解していないばかりに、意図せず剽窃をしてしまうことがありますので気をつけましょう。

ⓑ 要約

要約（**summary**）とは、長い文章の主旨をまとめたものです。*Oxford Advanced Learner's Dictionary* (7th ed.) では、"a short statement that gives only the main points of something, not the details" と説明されています。Paraphrase が元の文章の内容を別の表現で言い換えるのに対し、要約は論旨をとらえ、その要点を簡潔にまとめます。

要約の対象となるのは、本1冊であったり、その1章、数ページである場合もあります。また、学術雑誌の論文や新聞記事かもしれません。文献資料の種類にかかわらず、複雑な議論や多くの情報を扱う場合は、該当箇所をすべて抜粋したり、paraphrase するだけでは対処できません。このような時は、要約が必要になります。

要約を書く作業は2つの段階に分けられます。最初の段階では、対象となるテクストの論旨と論理的構成を把握します。次に、その趣旨を paraphrase の技術を活用して自分の言葉で表現します（この時、原文の一部をそのまま用いると直接引用の扱いになり、引用符が必要になります）。文献資料の情報を不正確に伝えてしまうと、論文の信頼性と説得力を損なうことになります。そうならないためにも、原文の内容を正確に理解し、正確かつ簡潔に表現することが重要です。

> 🔒 **要約のポイント**
> ・対象とする文章の論旨（main idea は何か、重要な supporting points は何か）を把握する。
> ・論旨を変えないように注意しながら、自分の言葉で表現する。Paraphrase と

> 同様、元の文章の表現をそのまま使わないようにする。Paraphrase のできない専門用語や論旨に深く関わる重要な語はそのまま使用してもよい。

Practice 1
Summarising

Read the following paragraph and write a summary.

> Although it is sometimes said that science is just another form of religion, this claim does not stand up to rigorous analysis. It is true that science and religion have some aspects in common. For example, they both attempt to explain the origin and nature of the universe and everything within it, including life itself. They are both the source of deep beliefs and both contain many mysteries, particularly in this age of quantum physics. However, science is different from religion in more important respects. Science is based on empirical evidence, and every scientific theory is judged according to its power of explanation and prediction of events in the material world. Science is continually trying to refute itself; it is always searching for the single piece of evidence that will disprove a theory, and a theory that is not able to be disproved by any evidence will never be taken seriously. By contrast, the central tenets of religion are by their nature unable to be proved or disproved by empirical evidence. They can be tested by no experiments, and they cannot be used to predict events in the material world. Though the two fields have some things in common, they are too fundamentally different for anyone to say that science is a form of religion.

Practice 2
Paraphrasing and Summarising

Read the following paragraph and answer the questions.

> One of the factors which affect the nature and quality of learning is whether motivation comes intrinsically or extrinsically. This distinction in the origin of motivation is based on the perception that the factors underlying motivation can be located either inside or outside a person. Thus, someone who is intrinsically motivated to learn about an academic subject is driven by his or her own interest in this subject and the sense that the learning experience in itself is enjoyable (Power 59-60). An extrinsically motivated student, however, does not have such inner reasons to strive for achievement. Instead he or she is influenced by external factors, such as grades or the perception that academic learning can lead to a well-paid job. In addition to the origin of motivation, the consequences of the two types are different: extrinsic information is often seen as the reason why learning is limited to surface approaches, whereas intrinsic motivation is associated with deep learning. Extrinsically motivated persons usually do not aspire to explore the subject further than necessary. As a result, their learning does not bring unexpected and inspiring discoveries. In contrast, someone who is intrinsically motivated is typically an active and engaged learner and therefore is more likely to obtain a broader as well as more profound knowledge of the subject. In conclusion, the origin of motivation is an important factor in determining the quality of the learning experience.

1. Paraphrase the sentences marked with a continuous underline. You should not copy the original text.
2. Paraphrase the sentences marked with a dotted underline. You should not copy the original text.
3. Write a summary of this paragraph.

SECTION 5　出典の示し方

　文献資料からの情報に論文で触れる場合は、それらが誰のものなのか、どこから入手したのか、つまり出典情報を明示しなくてはなりません。出典を示す第一の理由は、他人の知的財産を尊重するためです。逆に、出典を示さずに、他人の見解や意見、統計資料、実験結果などを用いることは剽窃に当たります。また出典を明示することで、論文の読み手が情報を共有できるようになります。これによって、読み手も文献資料を入手し、書き手の理解や解釈が正しいかどうかを判断することが可能になります。また、同じ文献や資料を、読み手も自分の研究で活用できるようになります。アカデミックな営為とは、議論を通じた知識の追求です。議論形成に重要な情報を共有することもその一部なのです。

　MLA 方式では、出典情報は 2 段階で明示します。最初に、論文中で文献資料からの情報に触れるたびに、本文中で出典を示します。これは、**in-text citations** と呼ばれます。次に、論文中で言及された文献資料すべてをリスト化し、詳細な情報を提示します。このリストは **Works Cited** と呼ばれ、論文の最終段落後に付します。これら 2 つを照合することによって、読み手は使用されている文献の出版情報を正確に把握することができるシステムになっています。そのため、in-text citations と Works Cited の情報が必ず一致するように留意します。

5-1　In-Text Citations

　MLA 方式では、出典は脚注ではなく、論文の本文中に含めます★2。具体的には、文章の末尾に括弧を置き、その中に出典情報を含めます。必要な情報は 2 点、著者名とページ数です。ただし、本文中で著者が明らかにされている時は、括弧内で改めて示す必要はありません。

★2　MLA 方式では、注の数は最小限にすることが奨励されていますが、他の書式では、出典情報を脚注や文末脚注で示すものもあります。

> **Example**

- There is the view that the government's radical reforms of the public sector will damage the slowly recovering economy of the country (Smith 5).
- Smith argues that the government's radical reforms of the public sector will damage the slowly recovering economy of the country (5).

　直接引用の場合は出典のページが特定されますが、広い範囲（数ページ、1つの章全体、文献全体など）を対象にした要約では、特定のページ数を挙げることができないことがあります。その場合は、in-text citations で章の番号（章全体の要約である場合）や著者名（文献全体の要約である場合）を挙げます。

> **Example**

- Before she embarks on a close-reading of the text, Blaire provides an overview of the critical history of the author (Ch. 3).
- He evaluates the major theoretical approaches available to analyse the phenomenon (Cameron).

　同じ論文中で同一の著者による資料を2つ以上使用している場合は、区別がつくように資料のタイトルも含めます。ただし、タイトルはすべて含める必要はなく、冒頭の数語以下は省略します。

> **Example**

- Brown called the government's move to dissolve the investigative committee as "one of the most unreasonable decisions that any government could ever make" ("Effective Measures" 63).

　著者が特定されていない場合は、資料のタイトルを挙げます。タイトルはすべて含める必要はなく、冒頭の数語以下は省略します。

- The government's recent decision to raise VAT has invited heavy criticism from public and private sectors ("The Government under Fire" 22).

★インターネット上の資料の扱い

　インターネット上に公開されている資料にはさまざまなタイプがあります。出典明示の際は以下を目安にしてください。
- Works Cited の該当項目の1番最初に現れる部分（著者名、記事名、ウェブサイト名、など）を挙げます。
- 印刷画面にした時のページ番号を挙げる必要はありません。

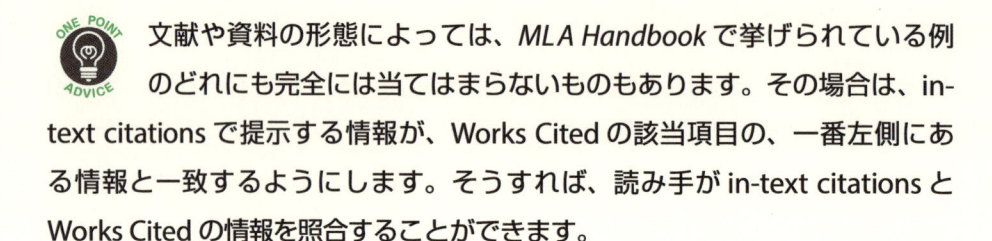

> **ONE POINT ADVICE**　文献や資料の形態によっては、*MLA Handbook* で挙げられている例のどれにも完全には当てはまらないものもあります。その場合は、in-text citations で提示する情報が、Works Cited の該当項目の、一番左側にある情報と一致するようにします。そうすれば、読み手が in-text citations と Works Cited の情報を照合することができます。

5-2　Works Cited

　前述したように、MLA 方式では in-text citations と Works Cited を照合することで、完全な書誌情報が得られるようになっています。ここで気をつけておくべきなのは、Works Cited とは、論文で実際に言及された文献資料のみを含むということです。よって、読んだけれども言及はしなかった「参考資料」は含めません。

Works Cited の書式と形式の基本

- 論文の最終段落の後、新しいページから始める。ページ上の中央に Works Cited と書く。ただし、文字をイタリック体にしたり、括弧を使う必要はない。
- 文献情報は、本文と同様ダブルスペースで記入する。各項目間に空白行を挿入した

- りしない。
- 各項目の2行目以降は半角5スペース分をインデントする。
- 学術雑誌所収の論文、新聞・雑誌記事など、所収ページが定まっているものはページ番号も挙げる。ページ番号が3桁以上で、始めと終わりの番号が下2桁のみ違う場合、終わりのページ番号は下2桁のみでよい。
- 文献資料の媒体を明記する。紙媒体であれば、「Print」、インターネット上のものであれば、「Web」と記す。
- 論文、書籍などのタイトルの各語の最初の文字は大文字にする（ただし、文頭にない冠詞、前置詞、等位接続詞、不定詞のtoは大文字にしない）。副題はコロン「:」の後に続ける。コロンの後はスペースを1つ空け、副題の最初にくる単語の最初の文字は大文字にする。
- 書籍や雑誌など、長いものはタイトルをイタリック体で表記する。詩や記事など短いものは引用符「" "」を使う。
- 著者（編者）名は、family name、middle name (middle initials)、first nameの順に書く。
- 著者名を基準として、全項目をアルファベット順に並べる。ただし、著者名が一番左端にない項目については、一番左端にある情報（例えば、文献資料のタイトル）を基準とする。

a 書籍

1. 著者が1人の書籍

Author's Name. *Title of Book*. Place of Publication: Publisher, Year of Publication. Medium of Publication.

Example

Canton, Ursula. *Biographical Theatre: Re-Presenting Real People?* Basingstoke: Palgrave, 2011. Print.

Deckard, Sharae. *Paradise Discourse, Imperialism, and Globalization*. London: Routledge, 2010. Print.

2. 編著者が 2 人以上の書籍
2 人目以降の編著者名は、first name、family name の順。

> **Example**
>
> Kenyon, Gary, Ernst Bohlmeijer, and William L. Randall, eds. *Storying Later Life: Issues, Investigations, and Interventions in Narrative Gerontology*. New York: Oxford UP, 2011. Print.

3. 同じ著者による複数の書籍
2 点目からは著者名を繰り返さず、3 つのハイフンを置く。ハイフンの間にはスペースを 1 つ置く。

> **Example**
>
> Byatt, A. S. *Possession: A Romance*. London: Chatto & Windus, 1990. Print.
> - - -. *Still Life*. London: Chatto & Windus, 1985. Print.

4. 企業や団体が作成した書籍など、個人の著者名がないもの
著者名の代わりに、企業や団体の名前を挙げる。

> **Example**
>
> American Psychological Association. *Publication Manual of the American Psychological Association*. 6th ed. Washington: American Psychological Association, 2009. Print.

5. 翻訳された書籍

> **Example**
>
> Foucault, Michael. *Madness and Civilization: A History of Insanity in the Age of Reason*. Trans. Richard Howard. London: Vintage-Random House, 1988. Print.

6. 日本語の書籍

著者名、タイトル、出版社名をローマ字表記で挙げる。タイトルはイタリック体で表記する。さらに、タイトルを英語に翻訳したものを [ ] 内に挙げる。

> **Example**
>
> Yaguchi, Yujin. *Hawai no Rekishi to Bunka* [*The History and Culture of Hawaii*]. Tokyo: Chuo Koron-Shinsha, 2002. Print.

7. 日本語に翻訳された書籍

> **Example**
>
> Eagleton, Terry. *Bungakutoha Nanika* [*What Is Literature?*]. Trans. Yoichi Ohashi. Tokyo: Iwanami-Shoten, 1997. Print.

8. 全集、論文集、事典などに所収の資料

Author's Name. "Title of Essay." *Title of Collection*. Ed. Editor's Name(s). Place of Publication: Publisher, Year. Page Numbers. Medium of Publication.

> **Example**
>
> Russo, Mary. "Aging and the Scandal of Anachronism." *Figuring Age: Women, Bodies, Generations*. Ed. Kathleen Woodward. Bloomington: Indiana UP, 1999. 20-33. Print.

ⓑ 定期刊行物

発行月は、May, June, July を除き、省略形にする。

Author's Name. "Title of Article." *Title of Periodical* Date Month Year: Page Numbers. Medium of Publication.

1. 雑誌記事

   Example

   Pearce, Eve. "Up to a Certain Point." *The Oldie* May 2011: 12-13. Print.

   月刊誌の場合は発行月のみでよい。

2. 新聞記事

   Example

   Fletcher, Nick. "A Spot of Fantasy Takeover Talk amid the European Turmoil." *Guardian* 11 Aug. 2011: 28. Print.

3. 学術雑誌記事

   Author's Name. "Title of Article." *Name of Periodical* Volume Number. Issue Number. Year of Publication: Page Numbers. Medium of Publication.

   Example

   Poyner, Jane. "Writing under Pressure: A Post-Apartheid Canon?" *Journal of Postcolonial Writing* 44.2 (2008): 103-14. Print.

c オンライン上の文献資料

　この Chapter の Section 1-2 で説明したように、ウェブ上の情報を使用する場合は、その情報が正確で信頼のおけるものか見極める必要があります。問題がないと判断した場合は、その他の文献資料と同じ方法で出典を示します。ただし、ウェブで入手できる資料にはさまざまなタイプがありますので、以下を基本的な目安としてください。

1. 著者名、編者名。
2. 記事のタイトル名を挙げ、二重引用符でくくる。
3. ウェブサイト、プロジェクト、書籍のタイトルをイタリック体で表記する。
4. もしも複数の版が存在する場合は、版の番号を記す。
5. 出版社情報（出版社名、出版日）（出版社名が不明の場合は「n.p.」、出版日が不明の場合は、「n.d.」と記入する）。
6. ページ番号（該当する場合）。
7. 出版媒体。
8. 資料にアクセスした日付（ウェブ上の情報は更新されることが多く、論文を執筆した時点にあった情報が、しばらく後に見つからないこともあります。そのために、その情報を参照した日付を記します）。

Web サイト全体

Editor, Author or Compiler Name. *Name of Site*. Version number. Name of Institution/Organisation Affiliated with the Site, Date of Resource Creation (if available). Medium of Publication. Date of Access.

Example

The Purdue OWL Family of Sites. The Writing Lab and OWL at Purdue and Purdue U, 2008. Web. 30 Mar. 2008.

Example

Works Cited

This is the Works Cited page of the model essay "Recognising the Many Dimensions of Academic Writing" in Chapter 3. See how the bibliographical details are presented and how they match the information given in the in-text citations.

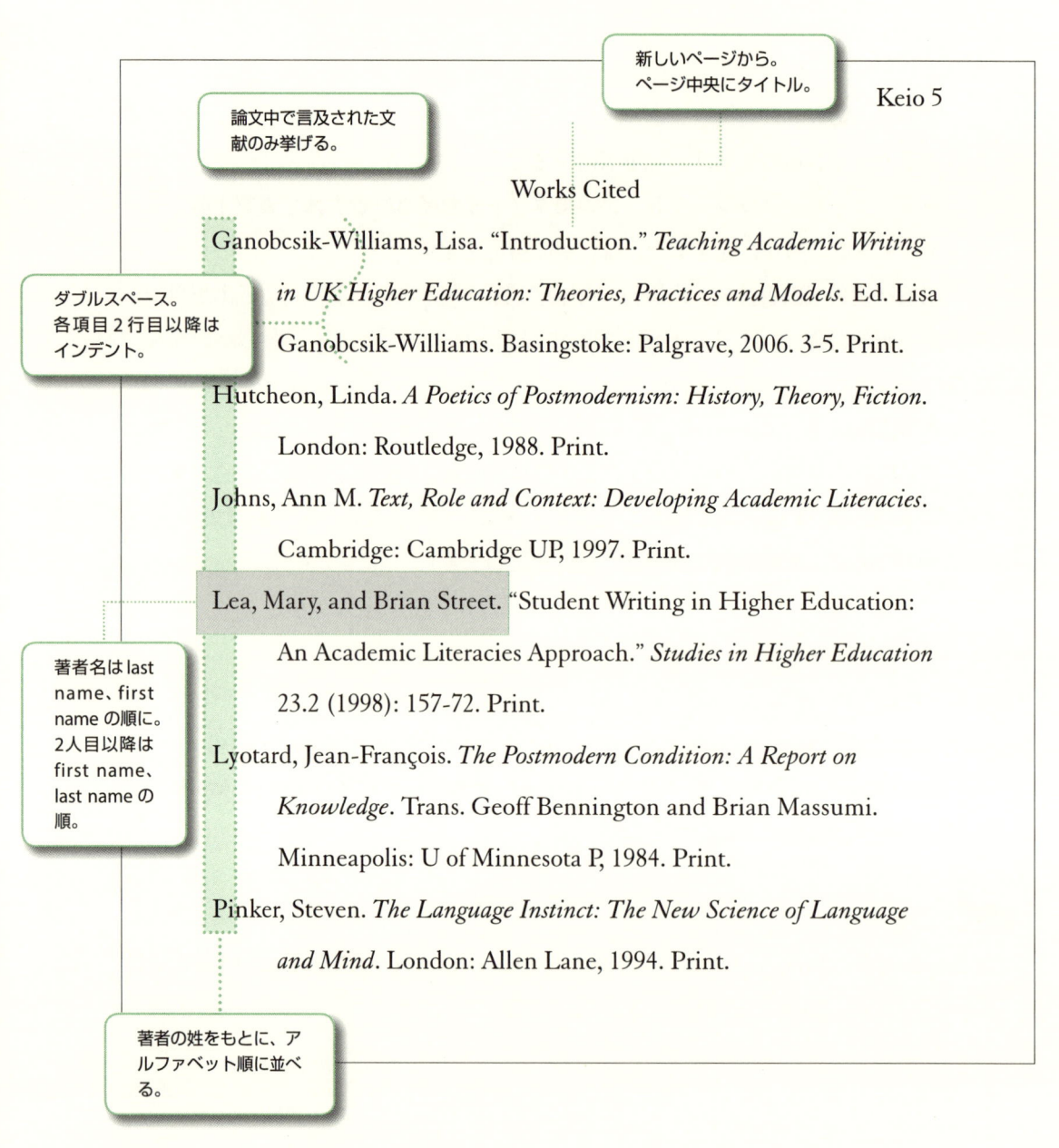

> Keio 5
>
> 新しいページから。
> ページ中央にタイトル。
>
> 論文中で言及された文献のみ挙げる。
>
> Works Cited
>
> Ganobcsik-Williams, Lisa. "Introduction." *Teaching Academic Writing in UK Higher Education: Theories, Practices and Models.* Ed. Lisa Ganobcsik-Williams. Basingstoke: Palgrave, 2006. 3-5. Print.
>
> Hutcheon, Linda. *A Poetics of Postmodernism: History, Theory, Fiction.* London: Routledge, 1988. Print.
>
> Johns, Ann M. *Text, Role and Context: Developing Academic Literacies.* Cambridge: Cambridge UP, 1997. Print.
>
> Lea, Mary, and Brian Street. "Student Writing in Higher Education: An Academic Literacies Approach." *Studies in Higher Education* 23.2 (1998): 157-72. Print.
>
> Lyotard, Jean-François. *The Postmodern Condition: A Report on Knowledge.* Trans. Geoff Bennington and Brian Massumi. Minneapolis: U of Minnesota P, 1984. Print.
>
> Pinker, Steven. *The Language Instinct: The New Science of Language and Mind.* London: Allen Lane, 1994. Print.

ダブルスペース。各項目2行目以降はインデント。

著者名はlast name、first nameの順に。2人目以降はfirst name、last nameの順。

著者の姓をもとに、アルファベット順に並べる。

CHAPTER 6

エッセイの構造 (2)

Section 1 | Introduction

1-1 Introductionの役割と構造

　人間の出会いでは、第一印象が相手に大きなインパクトを与えるといわれるように、論文も出だしが肝心です。読み手をいかに惹きつけるかは論文の大切な要素の1つで、その役割を担うのが序論にあたる **introduction**（あるいは introductory paragraph とも呼ばれる）です。そうはいっても、本論とは全く関係のない突拍子もない話題から始めてしまっては、読み手を困惑させるだけで、良い introduction とはいえません。読み手を惹きつけるということは、単に意外性やインパクトを与えることを意味するわけではありません。アカデミック・ライティングには型があり、introduction にも定式化された構造と役割があります。

　Introduction の一番重要な役割は、論文全体の主張を明文化した thesis statement を提示することです。しかし、いきなり thesis statement から始めることはしません。Thesis statement は論文の中で最も重要な部分ですが、読み手が論文のトピックについて知識を有しているとは限りません。このため introduction の導入では、トピックに関する背景的な情報などから始めて、thesis statement へとつなげていきます。まるで、濾過する時に使う漏斗の上部が広く、口先が狭くなっているようなイメージなので、このタイプの introduction は funnel introduction（漏斗型序論）と称されます（図3参照）。これは introduction の展開方法の中で最も標準的なものです。

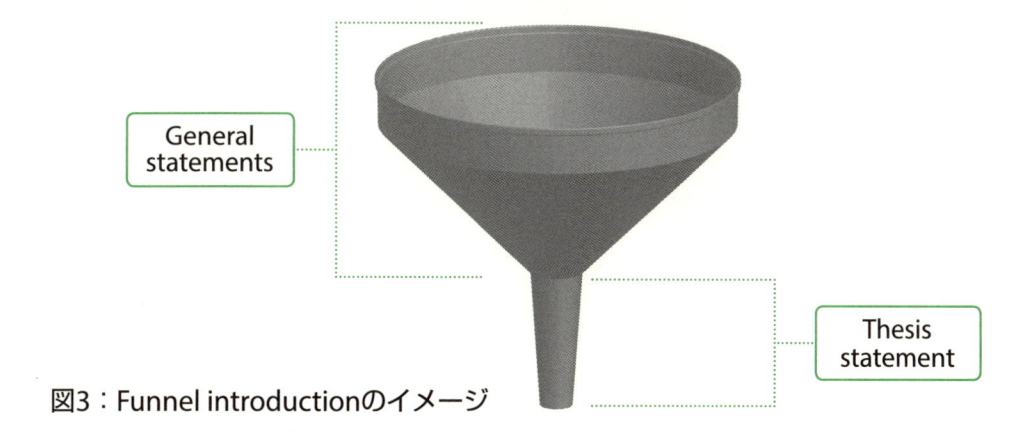

図3：Funnel introductionのイメージ

Funnel introduction は大きく分けて **general statements** と **thesis statement** から構成されています。最初に general statements において、論文のトピックを導入し、背景的知識を与えます。これによって、論文でどのような内容が展開されるのかを、読み手に予測させます。論文の意義や意図を示すのに必要な情報を提供し、徐々にトピックの焦点を絞り、最終的に thesis statement へとつなげていきます。顕微鏡を覗き込んだ時、特定のポイントにレンズのフォーカスを絞っていくかのように、general statements から thesis statement へと展開させていくのが理想とされています。

Introduction で論文の問いの背景や意義を説明する時、トピックに関する先行研究に触れることも効果的です。これは **literature review** と呼ばれます。ここでいう literature とは、文学ではなく、文献や論文を意味します。自分が扱うトピックに関する研究動向を示し、その中における自分のスタンスを位置づけたり、対象へのアプローチを示すことで、論文の目的や意義を浮かび上がらせます。学位論文、学術論文や学術書では introduction で literature review を行い、1 章をそれに充てることもあります。しかし、初学者が書くエッセイは短いことが多く、問いの設定が限定的な分、関わってくる学術的な議論も限られてきます。このため introduction で包括的な literature review を行う必要はあまりないでしょう。逆に、せっかく調べたからといって、本論とは関係のない情報まで含めず、thesis statement を導くのに必要な情報のみ提示しましょう。

Introduction の分量は、論文の長さによって異なってきます。例えば 1,500 words 程度のエッセイであれば、1 つのパラグラフに収めるのがよいでしょう。

1-2 Thesis Statementの重要性

Introduction において最も重要なことは、**扱う対象について、何を明らかにしようとするのか、結論を thesis statement として明示**することです。Thesis statement はトピックに関する書き手の主張を示す役割を果たし、英語論文・エッセイの要です。一般的に、introduction の最後で言明します。続く body で行うことは、この thesis statement がなぜ成立し得るかを論証していく作業に他なりません。ゆえに**明確な thesis statement を持ち、それを body で論理的かつ一貫性のある議論によって検証している**か否かが、優れたエッセイの鍵となります。

一般的に、thesis statement は次の要件を満たすことが求められます。

- 論文の長さに適した大きさのトピックを扱う。
- トピックに関して、書き手が学術的なリサーチから得た結論（thesis）を示す。1〜2文程度に収めるのが標準的。
- 第三者が検証可能な結論を示し、"I think〜"、"I feel 〜" といった表現を使わない（アカデミック・ライティングの表現に関してはChapter 1を参照のこと）。
- 単なる事実を述べたものであってはならない。
- 2つ以上の議論の方向性、可能性を持たせない。
- 単に論文で行うことや方針だけを述べることはしない（e.g. "I will analyse the influence of Japanese *anime* on contemporary French culture."）。

> **🔒 Introduction のポイント**
> 1. 読者にトピックと問い、アプローチなどを示す。
> 2. 論文の意図や意義を示すのに効果的な背景の説明や情報（先行研究など）を含める。
> 3. 必要以上の情報は含めない。
> 4. 結論を thesis statement として明示する（最終文で行うのが一般的）。

Practice

Read the sentences below and give a tick (✓) to each one you consider to be a strong thesis statement (for an essay of about 1,500 words). For the remaining thesis statements, give the reason for your low assessment by indicating (a) for containing fact only; (b) for being too broad; (c) for personal statements; (d) for having multiple ideas or arguments; or (e) for giving the direction of the argument only.

1. ____ Johannes Gutenberg invented the first printing press with movable type in the mid-fifteenth century.
2. ____ In Haruki Murakami's fiction human-animal hybrids are used as metaphor for the postmodern self.

3. _____ The illustrations of *Alice in the Wonderland* are fascinating.
4. _____ I will discuss Banana Yoshimoto's fiction and compare it to the work of Mariko Hayashi.
5. _____ Teaching English at primary school has both advantages and disadvantages.
6. _____ The Internet has had a tremendous impact on our lives and in recent years digital books have begun to change the way we read.
7. _____ Bathing has special connotations in Islamic culture.
8. _____ The concept of linking (*tsunagari*) is a key to success in marketing *Pocket Monsters* spin-off merchandise.
9. _____ I like the songs of Michael Jackson and I think they are the greatest in the history of pop music.
10. _____ The British royal wedding of Prince William and Catherine Middleton attracted worldwide public attention.

1-3　モデル・エッセイの分析

　Chapter 3 で読んだモデル・エッセイ "Recognising the Many Dimensions of Academic Writing" を使って、上で学んだ introduction のポイントを確認しましょう。

"academic writing" という大きなトピックを導入。ここではそのスキル習得に関する一般的な見解を紹介している。

エッセイのトピック（academic writing の習得）に関する背景的な情報や現状を提示。

> It is often assumed that **academic writing** is a primarily mechanical skill that students should be able to apply in any given context. For students who do not possess this ability, remedial classes should be offered to teach them how to write in proper sentences and use correct spelling and punctuation. In the UK separate study skills classes were usually offered to groups considered to be in particular need of such support: international and mature students as well as students from working-class families (Ganobcsik-Williams 3). This approach is still supported by many in the higher education system, but research in linguistics and **academic writing** has demonstrated that it is too simplistic. For instance the concepts of "academic literacies" and

General statements

"socioliteracy"—proposed respectively by Lea and Street, and Johns—highlight something necessarily more complex than a formal/technical practice. This essay argues that learning to **write academically** is indeed more complex than simply mastering the right vocabulary and the rules of syntax, spelling and punctuation.

Thesis statement

トピックに関する近年の研究者の見解を紹介。

上の先行研究を踏まえた書き手の見解（このエッセイで導き出す結論）を述べている。

　筆者は、冒頭で "academic writing" というトピックを提示し、このスキルは一度習得すれば、どのような場面にも適用できると考えられている、とアカデミック・ライティングの習得に関する一般的見解を紹介しています。次に、アカデミック・ライティングのスキルを持たない学習者には作文の技法を教授すべきで（第2文）、イギリスではそうした支援クラスが用意されているという、教育現場の現状に触れています（第3文）。そして、いまだに文法やスペリングなどの規則を教えることが重視され続ける中、最近の研究では、アカデミック・ライティングの性質がもっと複雑であるという見解が出されている点に触れ、トピックに関する先行研究の流れを押さえています（第4・5文）。そして最終文で、近年の研究に同意しながら、アカデミック・ライティングの学習は、語彙や文法習得だけに留まらない複雑なものであるという、筆者自身の見解（＝エッセイの結論）を提示しています。

　これらをgeneral statementsからthesis statementへという流れの中で押さえてみましょう。第1文で「アカデミック・ライティング」という大きなトピックを紹介し、第2〜3文でアカデミック・ライティングというスキルの「習得」へトピックを絞りながら、論文の指針を示しています（113ページのポイント1つめに当たります）。第3〜4文で、絞られたトピックに関する先行研究に触れ（ポイント2）、最終文でthesis statement として、このエッセイで筆者が最終的に述べようとする見解を提示する（ポイント4）、という展開が確認できます。一貫して、"academic writing"（の習得）をキーワードとしつつ、一般的見解から背景的な情報、そして書き手の主張へと絞り込むようにパラグラフを展開させています。これにより論理的かつ理解しやすい議論が構築されていることが分かります。

1-4　Introductionの作成で注意すべきこと

　先ほどのモデル・エッセイとは対照的に、初学者が作成したintroductionには、あまりにも広く漠然とした内容から始めたものや、introductionの中にunityのないものが多く見受けられます。また、thesis statementがなかったり、明確でないものや論文の方向性だけを説明したものもあります。

　次の文章は、"political blog"をトピックとして書いたエッセイ（1,500 words程度）のintroductionですが、改稿が必要です。Introductionとして何が不足しているのか、どこが不適切なのかを考えながら読みましょう。

　　　　A blog is a series of written accounts publicised and frequently updated on a website and written in an informal manner similar to a personal diary account. Blogs first appeared in the relatively early days of the Internet, the 1990s, and were largely personal accounts detailing people's daily lives. However, as website programs such as Open Diary in 1998 and Live Journal in 1999 became widely available, the number and popularity of blogs, first known as web journals, grew. The etymology of the term "blog" stems from the 1990s where it was first conceived of as a "web journal," which developed into "web log-weblog-wee blogs-blogs" (Tremayne vii). These early blogs were similar to diary accounts and developed into what is now commonly described as the personal blog which remains the most popular type. However, a plethora of different types of blogs has emerged, such as; corporate, civic, community, health and environment, technology and political blogs. In particular, the rise of political blogs on the Internet has had a widespread effect on mainstream media, and current research has illustrated that "the greatest impact on mainstream media comes not from personal journals but from political blogs," particularly, traditional print media such as newspapers (Tremayne x). As such, this paper will discuss the effects of political blogs on newspapers, focusing on

> both the advantages and disadvantages to assess whether or not the political blog will be the cause of death for this type of mainstream media.

　この introduction には、大きく分けて2つの問題点があります。1つめは thesis statement の中身です。筆者は、波線部の最終文を thesis statement として、このエッセイでは "political blog" が既存のメディアに与えた影響とその利点と欠点、そして現在の主要な報道メディアの存続の可能性を検討する、という問題提起をしています。しかし、thesis statement は論文で書き手が最終的に明らかにする結論を言明する文です。このため上の例のように、「この論文では〜について論じます」と方向性を述べただけでは、肝心な部分は曖昧で、thesis statement の要件を満たしていません。

　次に、general statements について検討してみましょう。読み手にも分かりやすいように、"blog" の概念を説明することで、一般的な内容で始めようという意気込みが感じられるものの、読み進めていくと、筆者の対象はより絞られたトピック "political blog" であることがわかります。これは thesis statement からも明らかです。ところが前半では、blog の定義、その登場の由来や種類といった説明にかなりの分量を費やしています。それに比すると、論文の主要トピックである political blog の扱いは簡潔すぎ、うまくバランスが取れていません。

　読み手に伝えるべき最重要箇所は thesis statement です。しかし、いきなり冒頭で論文の結論を提示しても、読み手がそれを理解するのは困難ですから、トピックに関する背景的な情報から始めます。とはいっても、この例のように thesis statement との関係からみて、大きすぎるトピックから始めてしまうのも問題です。冒頭で大きすぎる、あるいは多すぎる情報を与えてしまっては、読み手をうまく thesis statement へと導くことはできません。こうした混乱を避けるためにも、最初に明確な thesis statement をしっかり定めて、それに向かって焦点を絞っていくよう、冒頭から終わりまで introduction を構成しましょう。なお、この introduction の改稿例は、この Chapter の最後にある Review Exercises のエッセイを参考にしてください。

> 研究が進むにつれて新たな情報を得たり、当初の考えとは少し異なる解釈や見解が出てくることがあります。そのような場合、当然のことながら thesis statement を書き換える必要があります。執筆や研究を進めながら、常に論の方向性を確認して、必要に応じて thesis statement に修正を加えましょう。ただし、それに伴って introduction やアウトラインの修正も必要になるかもしれません。その際、論文内の一貫性を失わないようにしましょう。

SECTION 2　Body Paragraphs

2-1　Body Paragraphsの役割と構造

　エッセイにおいて introduction と conclusion に挟まれたパラグラフは body paragraphs（あるいは body）と呼ばれ、論文の展開を担う胴体部といえます。**Body paragraphs の役割は、introduction で提示された thesis statement の内容を論証すること**です。Thesis statement を詳しく説明し、具体的な事例や統計、専門家の見解を挙げ、関連する問題や事項を議論し、thesis statement の妥当性について読み手を説得します。

　各 body paragraph の構造は、独立パラグラフとほぼ同じです。つまり、パラグラフの main idea が topic sentence で明示され、続く supporting sentences によって詳細な説明や例示が行われます。しかし、body paragraph は独立した１つのパラグラフと異なり、concluding sentence が省略されることがあります。Body paragraphs の各パラグラフは、論文の議論を構成する複数ある論点の１つを提示するため、それだけで完結しているというよりも、次の論点を導く役割も果たしています。論理の流れが明確なように書かれていれば、concluding sentence がなくても、次のパラグラフへどうつながっているか、議論の流れが理解できるはずです。

　また、body paragraphs の数は、thesis statement に対する supporting points の数と必ずしも一致しません。１つの supporting point が何段階かの論理的展開を要するような複雑な内容の場合は、body paragraphs がいくつかセットになって、その supporting point

を説明している場合があります。また、1つの supporting point の説明で複数の例を挙げる時に、1つのパラグラフ内でそれらすべてを説明せず、複数のパラグラフに分けて各例の説明を丁寧に行うことがあります。この場合、結果的に1つの supporting point を複数のパラグラフで説明することになります。

2-2 エッセイにおけるTransition

　Chapter 2 で学んだように、パラグラフ内における議論の流れを読み手にわかりやすく示すことは重要です。そのために使われる表現は、transitional signals と呼ばれています。パラグラフよりも長い議論を提示するエッセイにおいては、論点のつながりを示し、読者を導くことはより重要になります。また、単一のパラグラフと比べると議論がさらに複雑になりますので、語や句単位の transitional signals を用いるだけでなく、文そのものに議論の流れを示す要素を含めることが多くなります。

　では、この Chapter の Section 1-3 と同じモデル・エッセイを使って、body paragraphs がどのようにつなげられているか確認しましょう。パラグラフ冒頭の数字は、エッセイ内で何番目のパラグラフに当たるかを示しています。
　以下は、introduction のすぐ後にくるパラグラフです。

(2)　　　The most important reason why writing in any context cannot follow rigid rules in a mechanistic way is the nature of language. Unlike the systems of communication used by animals, human language is not a finite set of expressions that babies learn and repeat. Instead it is a productive system, i.e. a system that allows speakers to say and understand "brand-new combinations of words, appearing for the first time in the history of the universe" (Pinker 22). In order to communicate via this system, speakers and writers have to be familiar with the rules that govern the use of a specific language. More than that, they have to be able to use them correctly in a specific context. This means that they cannot use a word

> or grammatical form in a single way whatever the context; instead they need to modulate their use in a way that is appropriate for the meaning they want to convey. Even if there are very stable rules for spelling, for instance, other aspects of language, such as the use of prepositions, vary greatly depending on the meaning a writer wants to express. For example, the verb "report" is not always followed by "to" (e.g. The employee had to report "to" his boss); the right preposition here could also be "on" (e.g. The employee had to report "on" his boss), depending on the context. The need to manipulate language flexibly to express the desired meaning is a crucial characteristic of human language that applies to all its uses, including academic writing.

　このパラグラフの前の introduction 末尾には次の thesis statement がありました。"This essay argues that learning to write academically is indeed more complex than simply mastering the right vocabulary and the rules of syntax, spelling and punctuation." 本パラグラフの topic sentence の破線部は、この thesis statement を paraphrase したものと理解できます。続く下線部はエッセイの最初の supporting point の内容を述べています。つまり、エッセイの最初の supporting point が、このパラグラフの main idea になっています。具体的には、アカデミック・ライティングが形式的な技術ではない理由の１つとして、言語の性質を挙げています。そして、専門家の意見や例を用いて、言語による意味の生産が、固定化されたルールに従うものでないことを説明しています。

　それでは、続く body paragraphs も検討してみましょう。それぞれの topic sentence が、どのように前パラグラフとのつながりを示しているか、また議論がどう展開されているかに注目してください。

> (3)　　　Another reason why acquiring simple rules about spelling, grammar and vocabulary is not sufficient to become a successful academic

writer is the fact that meaning does not exist in a vacuum. It is produced and received in specific situations and those who write and read take on specific roles (Johns 26). The importance of this social context can be easily observed in everyday situations: a student will speak one way to a university lecturer and another way to his or her friends, even if the topic is the same. Similarly, academic writing is shaped by the social context in which it takes place. Such texts reflect the norms of different academic fields in their structure and choice of vocabulary and grammatical forms.

前パラグラフ冒頭の "The most important reason" に呼応する形で、このパラグラフは "Another reason" という語句で始まっています。これが、このパラグラフで新たな supporting point が導入される合図の役割を果たしています。エッセイの thesis statement を支える2つ目の supporting point が本パラグラフの main idea に相当するわけです。Topic sentence にはそれを示す工夫がされています。まず、パラグラフ (2) と同様、topic sentence 前半（破線部）は thesis statement の内容を違う言葉で表現しており、supporting point の内容は、文後半（下線部）で説明されています。つまり、アカデミック・ライティングが固定化されたルールの集まりではない2つ目の理由として、言語の意味は文脈や状況に依存することを指摘しています。これを受けて、supporting sentences では、例や専門家の見解を引用し、社会的コンテクストによって、言語の使われ方が変化することを説明しています。二重線を引いた concluding sentence は、以上の内容を学問的なコンテクストに当てはめて、アカデミック・ライティングの文章も各学問分野の規範を反映していると述べています。

上の議論を受けて、続く2つのパラグラフはどのように展開しているでしょうか。

(4)　　In the English-speaking world the essay is a good example of the way in which text forms are influenced by the shared values of Anglo-Saxon academics. Good essays concentrate on a clearly defined topic that is introduced at the beginning. The argument is then developed through various paragraphs in the main body, before the logical conclusion is presented at the end. The overall structure, or macrostructure, of essays is thus clearly indebted to the Western philosophical tradition, which values linearity and a clear focus on a single topic more than lateral and associative thinking. The need to link paragraphs in a logical way also echoes Western traditions of thought (see, for example, Hutcheon 87). Although students can be taught to write an essay around a single topic, progressing from introduction, and body to conclusion, <u>it is more likely that they will succeed in this task if they are familiar with the ideas of logic and linearity</u>.

(5)　　　<u>In the same way it is easier for academic writers to choose appropriate vocabulary and grammatical forms</u> <u>if they are aware of the reasons why an academic community uses them</u>. A good example is the use of an impersonal style of writing. Academic texts tend to avoid referring directly to the writer ("I") or the reader ("you") and use many passive forms ("It has been shown" rather than "I have shown"). Many textbooks on academic writing introduce these forms as being essential for all forms of academic writing, but this generalisation overlooks the variation that can be found from one subject to another. The sciences are still dominated by the empiricist ideal of objectivity and, therefore, avoid almost any reference to individual persons (Lyotard). Postmodernist approaches in the humanities, on the other hand, argue that subjectivity is unavoidable; as a result, personal forms, such as I, are more often used in this field. The challenge for students is thus not only to learn how to write in an impersonal style, but also to explore how this is used in their specific field of study and why.

　パラグラフ（2）と（3）で挙げられたsupporting pointは言語の性質に関わる一般的な内容のものでした。それを踏まえ、パラグラフ（4）と（5）では、アカデミック・ライティングにより直接的に関わる事柄を議論しています。

パラグラフ（3）の concluding sentence は、パラグラフの main idea を学問的なコンテクストの中でとらえ、アカデミック・ライティングで奨励される形式や言葉使いが、学問分野の規範という、一種の社会的条件に規定されていることを指摘していました。パラグラフ（4）では、この典型例として、英語圏で一般的な essay の例を挙げています。Topic sentence 中の二重下線部は、前パラグラフ最後の二重下線部の内容を受けており、下線の部分が main idea を紹介しています。パラグラフ最後の concluding sentence（点線部）では、アカデミック・ライティングの文章形式の裏にある価値観（essay の例では、西洋的な論理と直線的思考）を知ることは、アカデミック・ライティング習得の助けになると言明しています。

　この内容を受け、パラグラフ（5）は "In the same way" という語句で始まっています。前パラグラフはアカデミック・ライティングの形式について議論していましたが、このパラグラフは、語彙と文法形式に焦点を当てています。Supporting sentences では、語彙が学問分野の価値観を反映する例として、代名詞「I」の使われ方を取り上げています。実証主義的な科学分野では主観性を示す「I」は使用されないが、人文学分野には主観性を不可避とみなす考え方があるため、その使用が許容されていると説明しています。この例を踏まえ、アカデミック・ライティングの学習者は、規範となる言語スタイルを形成する各学問分野の価値観を理解する必要があると述べています。

　では、次のパラグラフはどう展開していくでしょうか。

---

(6)　　　In addition to the values of an academic community, texts also reflect the social roles of writers and readers. Although these roles are rarely taught, understanding them is essential for academic writers in order to meet their readers' expectations. As with the use of impersonal forms, the social roles of writers and readers can vary from subject to subject, but also from culture to culture. This gives rise to a common problem for academic writers new to higher education in English-speaking countries. In some cultures respect for one's elders and their greater knowledge means that young academic writers are not allowed to engage critically

> with their sources and their lecturers' views; in contrast, lecturers in the English-speaking world expect their students to take a critical stance. They have to observe unwritten rules of politeness in their texts, but even relatively inexperienced academic writers can express criticism as long as it is supported by evidence. Discovering one's role as a writer or a reader in different contexts is, therefore, another important aspect of learning to write academically.

　先行する 2 つのパラグラフ（4）と（5）では、アカデミック・ライティングの規範は学術コミュニティーごとに定められていることが、具体例を通して示されていました。このパラグラフの topic sentence の点線部がそれを指しています。"In addition to" という表現により、これに加えて新たなポイントが導入されることを伝え、下線部でこのパラグラフの main idea（書き手や読み手の社会的な立場も、アカデミック・ライティングにおける言葉の選択、形式や内容などに関わってくる）が導入されています。そして続く supporting sentences で、英語圏外から英語圏に留学する学生の例を挙げることで、書き手の持つ文化的価値観が、その書き手が生み出すアカデミック・ライティングに影響を及ぼすことを説明しています。

🔒 Body Paragraphs のポイント

- Introduction で提示した thesis statement の supporting points を説明する。
- 各 supporting point と supporting detail がどのように関連しているのか、論理的つながりを示すことが重要。
- 各パラグラフの topic sentence に、前パラグラフとの論理的つながりを示す要素を含めることが多い。

SECTION 3 | Conclusion

3-1 | Conclusionの役割と構造

　Conclusion（あるいは concluding paragraph）とは、エッセイの主張を最後にもう一度確認するパラグラフです。論文全体が最後へ向かうことを読者に知らせるため、パラグラフの concluding sentence と同様、conclusion の冒頭では終わりを告げるシグナルを使います（Chapter 2、5-2 参照）。**Conclusion の主な役割は、thesis statement を言い換え、body paragraphs の要点を伝えること**です。通常、エッセイでは最終パラグラフが conclusion の役目を担います。

　それでは、モデル・エッセイの conclusion で上記のポイントを確認してみましょう。

終わりを告げる
シグナル

　In conclusion, the above discussion has demonstrated the impact of the social context on academic writing. The social roles and values of a community affect the practices of writing and, as a consequence, students cannot become successful academic writers unless they are aware of this context and know how to manipulate language to convey their intended meaning. This means that academic writing should not be considered as a separate, mechanistic skill that can be reduced to formal features, such as correct spelling or punctuation. Nonetheless, the teaching of rules to produce formally correct sentences is still dominant in higher education. This situation urgently calls for a new approach to academic writing, one that embraces its social dimension and truly helps students to become successful academic writers.

　結論部に入ることを "**In conclusion**" というシグナルで告げた後、それまでのパラグラフで論じてきたことを "the above discussion" という表現で受けながら、本論で展開してきた論の要旨（アカデミック・ライティングの習得には、社会的背景や所属する学術コミュ

ニティーが深く関わっており、学習者がそれを認識して理解することが大切である）を1行目の後半と2行目でまとめています。それらを踏まえて、次の文ではアカデミック・ライティングの学習において、形式的なことを学ぶだけでは不十分である、というthesis statementで述べた書き手の主張を言い換えています。続けて、そうした問題への認識がなされていないことを指摘し、現状の打開策の必要性に触れ、論文を締めています[3]。

3-2　Conclusionの作成で注意すべきこと

　日本人の初学者のエッセイには、conclusionこそ議論を展開させる場所だと勘違いしているものが少なくありません。しかし、エッセイの真髄であるthesis statementの論証を行うのはbody paragraphsで、conclusionはそれまでの内容を最後に確認する場所です。ゆえに、ここで**新たな論点を挙げたり、論証を展開させてはいけません**。Conclusionを書き終えた時、それがthesis statementと呼応しているか、そしてbody paragraphsで述べるべき内容を含んでいないかを必ずチェックしましょう。

> 🔒 **Conclusionのポイント**
> ・結論部に入ることを冒頭で示す。
> ・Introductionで提示したthesis statementの内容を再提示して確認する。あるいはエッセイ全体の要旨を示す。ただし、thesis statementは同じ言葉で繰り返さず、別の表現で言い換えること。
> ・新たな議論を導入しない。

---

[3] モデル・エッセイのように、conclusionの最後で明らかにされたことが関連分野に与える意義など、トピックについて今後考えるべき事柄をつけ加えることもあります。ただし、これは1〜2文程度に留めるようにしましょう。あまり詳しくたくさん書くとconclusionですべきでないこと、つまり新しい問題点や議論を持ち出すことになってしまいます。

Section 4 | Review Exercises

1. Read the essay below and answer the questions.

> Questions:
>
> 1. What is the topic of the essay? What is the thesis statement?
> 2. In the 2nd paragraph, replace incorrect nouns and pronouns so that the paragraph will demonstrate unity.
> 3. How many paragraphs does the body consist of?
> 4. How is the thesis statement developed in the body? List the points that develop the thesis statement.
> 5. Add transition words or phrases in the brackets.
> 6. Write a conclusion for the essay.
> 7. Give a title to the essay.
> 8. Reformat the "Works Cited" to comply with the MLA style (7th ed.).

While personal blogs remain the most numerous of all blogs, political blogs have increased in both popularity and influence in the new millennium, due in part to major political and social events such as the terrorist attacks of 11 September 2001, the Indian Ocean tsunami of 2004, and the London bombings of July 2007 (Tremayne xii; Gardner 16). Current research suggests that "the greatest impact on mainstream media comes not from personal journals but from political blogs" (Tremayne x). However, although political blogs have had a significant effect on mainstream media, they have not replaced the need for traditional journalism.

Political blogs have a number of advantages over the traditional mainstream media. They are almost always available free of charge and can be produced and accessed anywhere in the world, even in countries with strict censorship regimes. It can be updated continuously and flexibly as events develop, with no need to wait for a new edition or to rush for a deadline before all the facts are available. A political blog can provide information and points of view that may not be available in the mainstream media. Most importantly, we can present eyewitness accounts from people present at a major political or social event, where it may be impossible to send a mainstream reporter quickly, or at all, due to the interference of repressive regimes or unfamiliarity with local conditions. Taken together, these factors allow political blogs to publish first-hand accounts and photographic evidence of major events instantaneously throughout the world, often well before the mainstream media.

　　The mainstream media has reacted quickly to secure many of these advantages for itself. Major newspapers such as *The New York Times*, *The Financial Times*, *The Times* and *The Guardian* have extensive online versions of their print editions. Many of these online versions are available for free or offer free sections, and a growing number of them are developing exclusive online "news blogs" written by their journalists and updated from a variety of traditional and independent sources as major events unfold. (a.　　), during the recent demonstrations in Syria, President Bashar al-Assad and his government banned foreign journalists from entering the country, and news organisations such as the BBC called for eyewitness reports and relied on blogs to obtain detailed first-hand information on the situation. All of these changes demonstrate the significant effect that political blogging has had on the mainstream media.

　　(b.　　), political bloggers have a number of important shortcomings when compared to the mainstream media. Most of them rely on donations or limited advertising for their revenues, and do not have the resources available for a wide range of original investigative journalism. They may not be able to afford to travel, and can only report on events that happen around them. They may not be granted press credentials and can rarely take advantage of the contacts or reputation that a mainstream media organisation can use to gain access to people or information. (c.   ), most political blogs offer a great deal of opinion and analysis but less frequently provide facts or original investigative journalism. Instead, they remain heavily dependent on the mainstream media for their primary sources. Research has shown that "the most common types of links found in blog posts are links to mainstream media" (Tremayne 261), illustrating the need for newspaper articles as a basis for the political blogs' opinions and reports. *The New York Times* website tracks and publishes data on its "most blogged" articles, encouraging the symbiotic relationship between political blogs and newspapers but establishing traditional newspapers at the centre of this relationship.

Perhaps the greatest disadvantage faced by political blogs is the difficulty of establishing and maintaining credibility. Instantaneous blogging often means inadequate fact-checking, and bloggers are rarely as accountable as the mainstream media, with few consequences for publishing inaccurate or misleading information. This is particularly the case when so many blogs are anonymous or pseudonymous. (d.   ), in 2011 the blog "A Gay Girl in Damascus," apparently written by a Syrian girl called Amina Abdallah Aral al Omari, attracted worldwide attention during the fraught political situation in Syria; the blogger was thought to have been captured by the Syrian armed police, raising great concern for her safety. The revelation of the blogger's true identity as a male American student at Edinburgh University, Tom MacMaster, did considerable damage to the credibility of blogging as a news source, and had additional consequences for the gay activists in Syria who had believed in the fictional Amina and her political reporting.

It is difficult to see how the disadvantages faced by political blog sites can be overcome. With the world's most successful media organisations still struggling to generate money from the Internet, heavily subsidising their online operations using traditional revenues, it is unlikely that independent bloggers will be able to access sufficient resources to generate substantial original reporting. Though many individual bloggers may together provide a range of news and opinion, they will always lack the coordination and efficient allocation that can be provided by a single news desk. Although individual bloggers may develop a degree of reputation and credibility, every blogger has to establish that credibility from zero: they have no access to the institutional reputations of respected mainstream news organisations. Indeed, it may be that the very aspects that make blogging most valuable, such as independence, local access and even insider knowledge, will always put it at a disadvantage compared to the mainstream media.

Works Cited

Tremayne, Mark. Harnessing the Active Audience: Synthesizing Blog Research and Lessons for the Future of Media. *Blogging, Citizenship, and the Future of Media*. Mark Tremayne. ed. 2007. London: Routledge. 261-272.

Tom MacMaster. "A Gay Girl in Damascus. *Blogspot.com*. Blogger. 19 February 2011. Web. 7 July 2011

Gardner, Susannah, and Shane Birley. *Blogging for Dummies*. Hoboken: Wiley Pub. Co. 2008.

2. Below is an incomplete outline of the essay you have just read above. Complete the outline by filling in the missing parts.

Outline

Title: _____

I. **Introduction**

   Thesis Statement: Although political blogs have had a significant effect on mainstream media, they have not replaced the need for traditional journalism.

II. **Body**

   A. Political blogs have a number of advantages over the traditional mainstream media.
   1. They are cheaply and easily accessible.
   2. They are continuously and flexibly updated.
   3. They provide information and opinion that may not be available in the mainstream media.
   4. They provide eyewitness accounts from people on the ground.

   B. The mainstream media has adapted to secure these advantages for itself.

1. _____
2. Many online newspapers now have blog sections linked to a range of other sources.

C. _____

1. They do not have the resources for much original investigative journalism.
    a. Travel.
    b. _____
    c. Contacts and reputation.
2. _____
    a. Most links in blog posts are to mainstream media.
    b. Most blog posts consist of analysis or opinion rather than factual reporting.
3. They have limited credibility.
    a. _____
    b. They are often anonymous or pseudonymous.

D. _____

1. Limited access to revenues.
2. Limited ability to coordinate.
3. _____

III. Conclusion

CHAPTER 7

完成に向けて

Section 1 書式

　Chapter 1 で説明したように、アカデミック・ライティングでは、内容だけでなく形式も重要です。よって、アカデミックな論文にふさわしい、正確で客観的な語彙や表現を用いる必要があります。また、論文で言及された文献資料の情報を読み手が正確に把握できるよう、引用の仕方や書誌情報の提示形式が分かりやすく、統一されていることも重要です。そこで Chapter 5 では、本書が依拠するスタイル例として MLA 方式について学びました。

　この Chapter では、MLA で示されている書式に関するガイドラインについて学びます。他の形式面と同様、書式についても MLA 発行の *MLA Handbook for Writers of Research Papers* で詳細に説明されています。ただし、情報量が多いので、ここでは、本書の利用者に特に関連があると思われる基本的な事項のみを紹介します。また、日本の事情に合わせて変更している事項がありますので、注意してください。ここに説明がない事項については、*MLA Handbook for Writers of Research Papers* の最新版（2014 年 1 月現在、第 7 版が最新版）を参照してください。

書式の基本事項

- 特に指定がなければ、A4 サイズの紙を使用する。
- 手書きはせず、コンピューターで作成する。
- 原稿すべて（引用、注、Works Cited 含む）をダブルスペースにする。
- 原稿は左揃えとする（つまり、行の右端を揃える必要はない）。
- ピリオドなど、文章を終える句点の後は、半角スペースを 1 つ置く。
- 文章中のコンマやコロン、セミコロンの後も、半角スペースを 1 つ置く。
- フォントのサイズは 12 ポイント。フォントの種類は読みやすいもので、標準とイタリック体の区別がはっきりしているものを使う。標準的なフォントは Times New Roman など。
- ページの上下左右には余白を入れる。MLA 指定の余白幅は、左右上下とも 1 インチ（約 2.5 センチ）。

- ページ番号はページ右上、上辺より 0.5 インチの場所に配置。1 枚目からページ番号を 1 から振る。番号の前には自分の名字をつける。名字と番号の間にはスペースを 1 つ挿入。番号の前に「p.」を入れたり、後にピリオドを添えたりする必要はない。
- 表紙は不要。
- 1 ページ目、左上に自分の名前と日付をダブルスペースで記入。改行し、タイトルをページ中央に配置。さらに改行し、本文を開始する。
- タイトルは太字、イタリック体で表記したり、下線を引いたり、括弧に入れたりしない。ピリオドを添える必要はない。
- 見出し（Works Cited 等）にピリオドを添える必要はない。
- 引用符は「" "」、引用符の中に引用符がある場合は「' '」を使う。
- コンマやピリオドは引用符の中に入れる。
- 長い作品（長編映画、小説、書籍、新聞、雑誌など）のタイトルはイタリック体にする。また、各単語の最初の文字は大文字にする（冠詞、前置詞、等位接続詞は除く）。
- 短い作品（雑誌新聞記事、詩、随筆など）のタイトルは引用符に入れる。

Practice

Correct formatting errors in the following texts.

1. The change in the national curriculum in 1992 marked 'a definitive turning point'. (Baker, 88)
2. One critic concludes, "It was one of her earliest poems, "After The Worst" that testifies to her extraordinary visual imagination" (Springfield 5).
3. Everyone was fascinated when Mr Obama, a presidential candidate at that time, exclaimed, "CHANGE."
4. According to an article in the "Asahi Shimbun," scientists have found evidence that a lack of sleep is one of the contributing factors for weight gain.
5. The article raises the question, "Is it really necessary to teach English at primary school"? This uncertainty is shared by many who work in primary school education.

ONE POINT ADVICE　セクション分けについて

　長い論文では、議論のまとまりごとに、本文を章やセクションで分けることがあります。しかし、区切りを設けてタイトルをつけただけで、本文中で論の展開の説明を行っていないものを多くみかけます。これでは、各セクション間の議論の連続性を理解することが大変難しくなります。本来は、区切りや区切りごとのタイトルがなくても、議論の流れが分かるように論文が書かれていなければなりません。つまり、たとえセクションごとにタイトルがあったとしても、「今までは△について×××といってきた、だから、次は○について□□と示す必要がある」というように、論理の流れを読み手に分かりやすく説明する必要があります。エッセイのように短い論文では、本文を細かく区切ることは好ましくありません。長さが短いということは、必然的に議論の焦点がかなり絞られます。したがって、セクション分けをしなくても、本文中で流れを説明するだけで、読み手には十分理解ができるはずです。論文の本論を内容のまとまりごとに分けることは時には必要ですが、セクションのタイトルに議論の流れを指し示す仕事を肩代わりさせてはいけません。

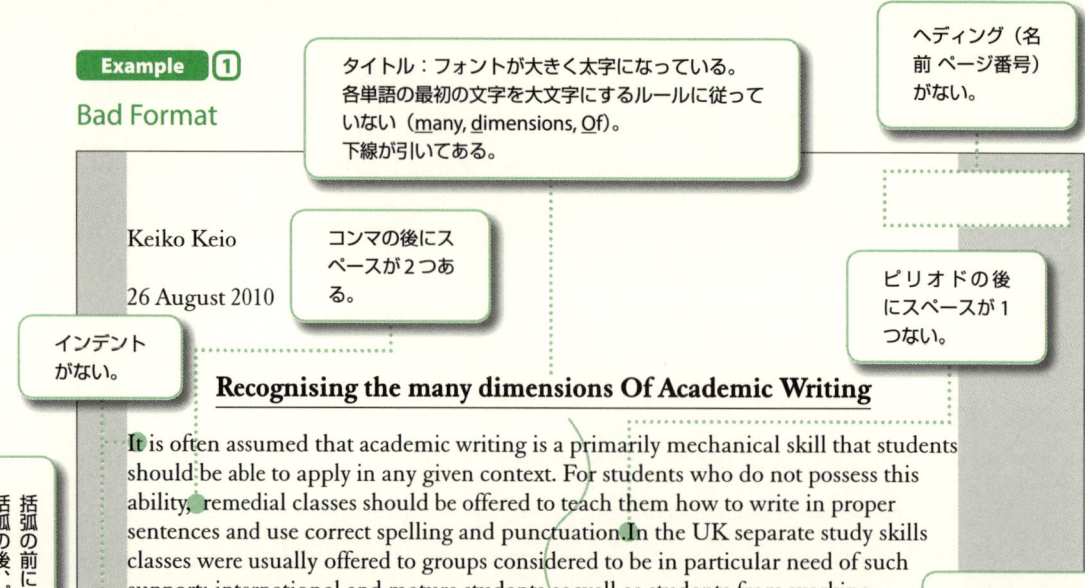

Example 1

Bad Format

Keiko Keio

26 August 2010

Recognising the many dimensions Of Academic Writing

It is often assumed that academic writing is a primarily mechanical skill that students should be able to apply in any given context. For students who do not possess this ability, remedial classes should be offered to teach them how to write in proper sentences and use correct spelling and punctuation.In the UK separate study skills classes were usually offered to groups considered to be in particular need of such support: international and mature students as well as students from working-class families(Ganobcsik-Williams 3) . This approach is still supported by many in the higher education system, but research in linguistics and academic writing has demonstrated that it is too simplistic. For instance the concepts of "academic literacies" and "socioliteracy"–proposed respectively by Lea and Street, and Johns– highlight something necessarily more complex than a formal/technical practice. This essay argues that learning to write academically is indeed more complex than simply mastering the right vocabulary and the rules of syntax, spelling and punctuation.

The most important reason why writing in any context cannot follow rigid rules in a mechanistic way is the nature of language. Unlike the systems of communication used by animals, human language is not a finite set of expressions that babies learn and repeat. Instead it is a productive system, i.e. a system that allows speakers to say and understand "brand-new combinations of words, appearing for the first time in the history of the universe." (Pinker 22) In order to communicate via this system, speakers and writers have to be familiar with the rules that govern the use of a specific language. More than that, they have to be able to use them correctly in a specific context. This means that they cannot use a word or grammatical form in a single way whatever the context; instead they need to modulate their use in a way that is appropriate for the meaning they want to convey. Even if there are very stable rules governing, for instance, other aspects of language, such as the use of prepositions, may vary greatly depending on the meaning a writer wants to express. For example, the verb "report" is not always followed by "to" (e.g. The employee had to report "to" his boss); the right preposition here could also be "on" (e.g. The employee had to report "on" his boss), depending on the context. The need to manipulate language flexibly to express the desired meaning is a crucial characteristic of human language that applies to all its uses, including academic writing.

Good Format

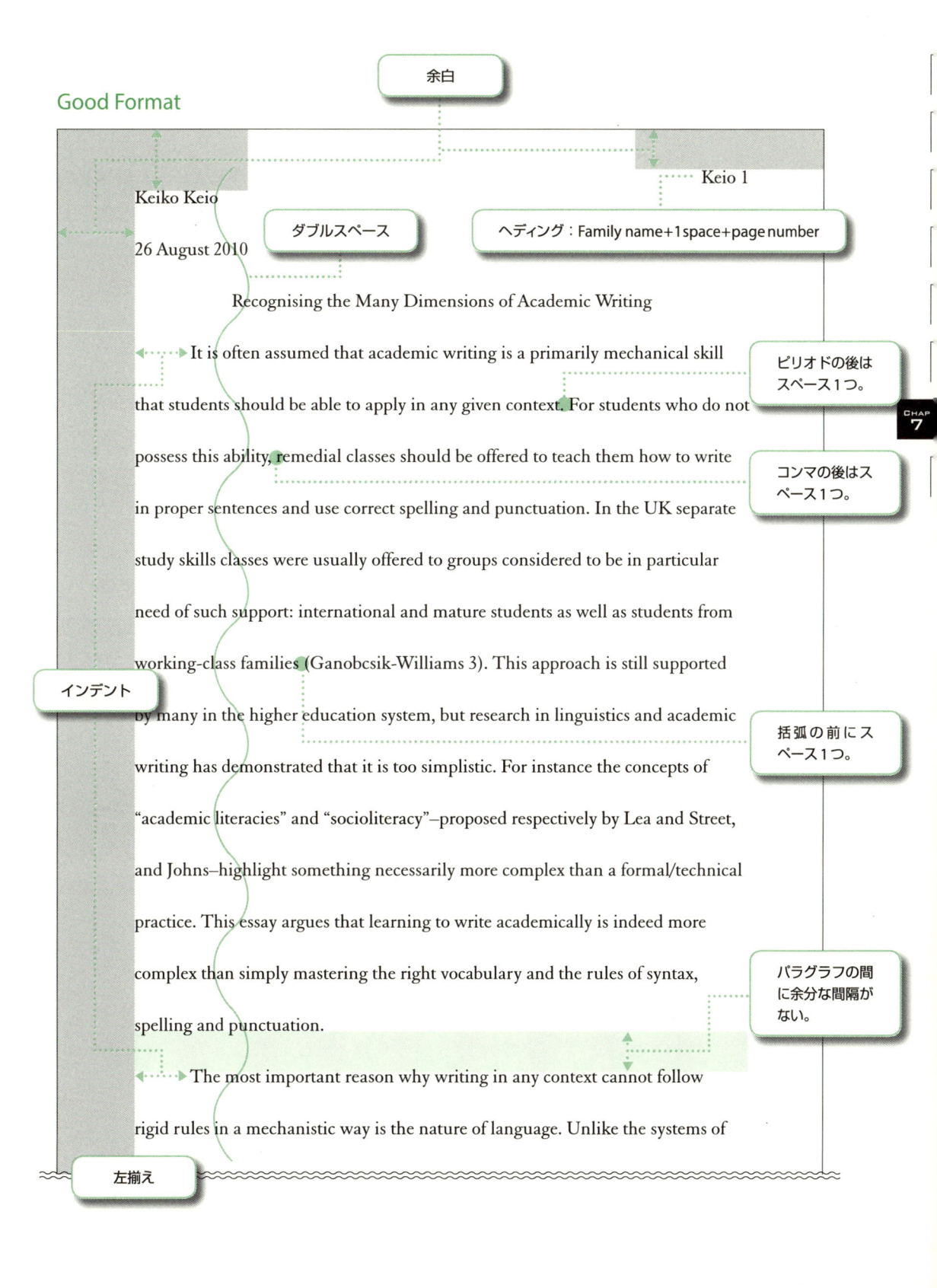

Keiko Keio

26 August 2010

Recognising the Many Dimensions of Academic Writing

    It is often assumed that academic writing is a primarily mechanical skill that students should be able to apply in any given context. For students who do not possess this ability, remedial classes should be offered to teach them how to write in proper sentences and use correct spelling and punctuation. In the UK separate study skills classes were usually offered to groups considered to be in particular need of such support: international and mature students as well as students from working-class families (Ganobcsik-Williams 3). This approach is still supported by many in the higher education system, but research in linguistics and academic writing has demonstrated that it is too simplistic. For instance the concepts of "academic literacies" and "socioliteracy"–proposed respectively by Lea and Street, and Johns–highlight something necessarily more complex than a formal/technical practice. This essay argues that learning to write academically is indeed more complex than simply mastering the right vocabulary and the rules of syntax, spelling and punctuation.

    The most important reason why writing in any context cannot follow rigid rules in a mechanistic way is the nature of language. Unlike the systems of

Section 2　推敲

　論文作成はプロセスです。しかも、一直線に進むプロセスではありません。トピックを定め、問いを設定し、文献資料を調べ、アウトラインを練り、それに沿って全体を書き上げますが、この工程の一部を何度も繰り返したり、予定を変更したりすることは珍しくありません。例えば、書き始めてから、アウトラインがうまくできていないことに気づいたり、よりよいアウトラインが浮かんだり、新しい資料を見つけたり、いろいろな理由で修正や書き直しが必要になることはよくあることです。

　さらに、この繰り返しのプロセスの山場は、実は、全体を書き上げた後の推敲の作業です。一旦書き終えた論文を冷静に読み返すことで、表現の正確さだけでなく、論証の客観性や論理性、論文の読みやすさを高めることができます。読み返す際には、読み手の視点に立つことが重要です。読み手に分かりにくい箇所はないか、論理的つながりが分かりやすく書かれているか、提供している情報（説明）は十分か、逆に不要な情報が含まれていないか、などに注意を払います。全体の議論が整ったら、表現も検討します。もっと簡潔に分かりやすく書けないか、1つの文章やパラグラフが長すぎないか、同じ表現や語句の繰り返しがないか、自分の書いたものを吟味します。読み返す際には、自分の書いたものを客観的に読む必要があるため、数時間、できれば数日おいて読み直すのが望ましいでしょう。これらの作業を英語では revision や rewriting といいます。Proof-reading もよく使われますが、これは日本語の「校正」に近い意味で、revision や rewriting の終了後、最終的な原稿に誤字脱字やタイプミスなどの誤りがないかを確認する作業を指します。右ページの例は、Chapter 2 に含まれるモデル・パラグラフが完成する前の原稿の例です。ただし例として、revision や rewriting の段階と proof-reading の段階の推敲箇所が両方含まれています。

　推敲の際には、次の Section のチェックリストを活用しましょう。

Example 2

The Benefits of Working Summer Time Hours in Japan

In recent years the introduction of "summer time" working hours ~~is~~ **has been** hotly discussed **in Japan**. In this model, the conventional working day of 9–5 is shifted so that workers start and finish a couple of hours earlier. ~~Should companies employ summer time hours?~~ **[Write a thesis statement.]** Firstly, it hel~~p~~s **will help** them to reduce electricity consumption. Summer temperatures can be intolerably high during the day. But it is relatively cool in the early morning. **[Combine sentences]** If ~~they~~ **workers** take advantage of the cooler morning hours, this will mean air-conditioning is used less. Summer time hours are g~~oo~~d in **[Use a more precise word]** **[Add a transitional signal.]** reducing electricity for lighting, because the workers finish work and leave the office before it gets dark. In addition to reduced power consumption, summer time hours can m~~a~~ke **increase** workers' productivity hig~~h~~er. Overtime has long been part of Japanese corporate culture; the topic of notoriously long working hours is frequently brought up in foreign media. ~~Its~~ **It is** likely, however, that the introduction of summer time hours will put pressure ~~to~~ **on** companies to increase their workers' productivity and operational efficiency. ~~B~~**b**ecause the expected **This is** benefits of summer time hours will completely l~~o~~**be**se **lost** if workers start earlier but continue to work late. Finally, summer time hours will allow workers to keep their work-life balance. **[Add examples.]** In short, the introduction of summer time hours should be highly beneficial for Japanese companies in terms of improved energy-saving, productivity and employees' work-life balance.

SECTION 3 チェックリスト

　本書ではエッセイの作成のために理解すべき、アカデミック・ライティングの特質及び要件、形式を説明してきました。それらの重要項目を以下のチェックリストにまとめました。自分が書いた論文を読み返して編集する際に役に立ててください。質の高い論文を生み出すために、すべての項目が満たされているか、丁寧に確認しましょう。

Essay Checklist

	Formatting	
1	There is a margin on all four sides of the paper.	
2	The essay is double-spaced throughout.	
3	The font size is 12 points.	
4	The title of the essay is centred on the first page of the essay. The title is appropriately capitalised.	
5	There is an indentation at the start of each paragraph.	
6	The author's family name and the page number are placed in the top right corner of each page, in line with the right edge of the body text.	
7	There is a period at the end of each sentence, followed by one space.	
8	The commas are followed by one space.	
	Academic Style	
1	There are no spelling errors and grammatical mistakes.	
2	The essay is written with vocabularies and expressions which are suitable for academic work.	

		Essay Structure	
	1	The essay follows the outline and has introduction, body and conclusion.	
	2	There is a clear thesis statement in the introduction.	
	3	The conclusion restates the main idea of the essay and summarises the major supporting points.	
		Paragraph Structure	
	1	The essay's argument is presented in a series of structured paragraphs.	
	2	A paragraph contains one topic and one main idea.	
	3	A paragraph has a topic sentence, which clearly states the main idea of the paragraph.	
		Coherence, Unity and Persuasiveness of Argument	
	1	The topic is sufficiently narrow. The question to be addressed is clearly framed.	
	2	The essay presents one unified argument/view about the question.	
	3	There is unity and coherence throughout the essay.	
	4	The logic of the argument is clearly indicated using transitional signals.	
	5	The argument is supported by objective data such as examples, experts' opinions or statistics.	
	6	There is a clear distinction between the author's own opinions and those of others.	
		Research: Use of Sources	
	1	All the external materials are cited in MLA style, in the form of direct quotation, paraphrase, or summary.	
	2	All the external materials are referenced in MLA style (in-text citations).	
	3	All the external materials which are cited in the essay are listed in Works Cited, following MLA style.	

SECTION 4　モデル・エッセイ

次の指示に従って、モデル・エッセイを読みましょう。
1. アウトラインを参考に、議論がどのように構成されているかを意識して読みましょう。
2. 前ページチェックリストの項目が満たされているかを確認しましょう。

Outline

The Need for Electoral Reform in the United Kingdom

I. Introduction

Thesis statement: The United Kingdom's electoral system is badly outdated and in urgent need of reform.

II. Body

　A. The UK system is a "first past the post" system or "single-member district plurality" system.
　　1. Every constituency or district is represented by only one member.
　　2. Each voter votes for one candidate.
　　3. The candidate with the highest number of votes wins.

　B. This system has significant disadvantages.
　　1. Many voters have no representation in parliament.
　　2. Some parties' representation may not reflect their popular support.
　　3. Similar candidates can split the vote.
　　4. Tactical voting.
　　5. It leads to a two-party system thanks to Duverger's Law.

　C. There are many other alternatives available.
　　1. Alternative vote.
　　2. Proportional representation.
　　3. Many other combinations and variations.

D. Many other elections take advantage of these alternatives.
  1. Different countries.
  2. Different elections within the UK.

III. **Conclusion**

The UK should reform its electoral system and improve democracy for all its citizens.

Model Essay

Fukuzawa 1

Yukichi Fukuzawa

29 January 2008

エッセイの主張が伝わるタイトル。タイトルは文でなく名詞形。

The Need for Electoral Reform in the United Kingdom

Thesis statement につながる形でトピックを導入

The United Kingdom's general election of May 2010 yielded results that surprised many observers, particularly outside the country. The centre-left Labour and left-wing Liberal Democrat parties together won the most seats and the majority of votes, but the government was formed by the centre-right Conservative party. The left-wing Liberal Democrat party performed much worse than the polls predicted, and won only a fraction of the seats despite broad popular support across the country. These perverse results did not arise through chance but were caused by structural defects in the United Kingdom's electoral system, which is badly outdated and in urgent need of reform.

代名詞を的確に用いてcoherenceを持たせる。

Thesis statement でエッセイの主張が述べられている。

Fukuzawa 2

The United Kingdom's electoral system is often described as a "first past the post" system, or more technically as a "single-member district plurality" system. Under this system, the whole of the United Kingdom is divided into 650 geographical districts or constituencies, each representing around 70,000 eligible voters. Every constituency elects exactly one member to a seat in the House of Commons. Voting is very simple: each voter casts a single vote for one of the constituency's candidates, most of whom belong to a political party, and the candidate with the highest number of votes wins the seat. The winner is not required to win a majority or any minimum percentage of the votes, only more votes than any other candidate. Thus, for example, in 2010 the Liberal Democrat candidate won the seat of Norwich South with only 29.4% of the votes—the lowest in the general election ("Election 2010"). In these situations, the "first past the post" description may be misleading, since there is no real "post," which is why the technical description of a single-member district plurality system is sometimes preferred (Loenen 157).

However it is described, the current system has a number of

significant disadvantages. First, a great many voters may consider that they have no influence or representation in the parliament. In an electorate such as Norwich South, fully 70.6% of the voters did not vote for their representative. If these patterns are repeated across the country, a majority of voters may find they have no say in the composition of the government. Similarly, a political party's representation in the parliament may be out of all proportion to its support across the country. For example, in the 2010 general election the Liberal Democrats won 23% of the votes but only 7.8% of the seats, while Labour won only 29% of the votes but 39.6% of the seats ("Election 2010"). Many voters find these discrepancies disheartening. Further, the presence of two similar candidates on the same ballot can split the vote with unrepresentative results: for example, two left-wing candidates may each receive 30% of the vote, resulting in the election of a right-wing candidate with 40% of the vote. The 60% of electors who voted for one of the left-wing candidates are unlikely to be happy with this outcome. Many voters try to avoid this situation by "tactical voting": that is, voting not for their preferred candidate, but for a candidate they think has a chance of winning. As a result of all these factors, smaller parties have even less chance of gathering significant electoral support, leading to the domination of the political landscape by two major parties. This tendency has become known as Duverger's Law after being identified by Maurice Duverger (23-32). A system that can generate such perverse outcomes clearly suffers from many significant drawbacks.

There are many alternative systems available. One model, which was proposed after the 2010 election, is known as the "alternative vote" system. Under this system, a single representative is still elected from each constituency; but instead of simply casting one vote for one candidate, voters are asked to rank the candidates in order of their preference. For example, an elector might vote first for a left-wing candidate, second for a centre-left candidate, and third for a right-wing candidate. If no candidate wins more than half of the first-preference votes, the lowest-ranked candidate is eliminated and his or her votes are distributed according to the second preferences of the people who voted for him or her; and this process is repeated until one candidate has more than half of the votes. As a result, voters can cast their primary votes for candidates who have a low chance of winning, safe in the knowledge that their votes will be transferred to their second preferences if necessary. This eliminates the need for tactical voting, prevents similar candidates from splitting the vote, and gives smaller parties more of a chance to attract support. However, since it still elects only one candidate for every seat, it may not eliminate the problem of some candidates winning tens of thousands of votes in a constituency, or parties winning millions of votes nationwide, but missing out on seats in parliament. To mitigate this issue, some form of proportional representation is required. A proportional system removes the limit of one representative per constituency: it may introduce larger geographical constituencies with multiple representatives, or it may allocate additional seats in the parliament on the basis of national rather than constituency representation. There are many combinations and variations of these principles, including the block vote, the party block vote, the two-round system, the single transferable vote, the single non-transferable vote, the mixed-member proportional system,

> 議論の流れを示す transitional signal。

the limited vote—and the Borda count used only on the tiny island of Nauru. One of these alternatives must be preferable to the very blunt and imprecise system used in the United Kingdom today. In fact, Anthony Gottlieb argues that "it's clear that no country would pick first-past-the-post voting today."

Indeed, alternative electoral systems are now widespread throughout the world, with the United Kingdom, the United States and Canada unique among OECD nations in clinging to the "first past the post" system for their main houses of parliament. The "alternative vote" proposed after the 2010 election is very similar to the preferential voting system used in Australia since 1918. Most of Europe and South America, as well as Japan and New Zealand, use some form of proportional representation, most commonly party-list proportional representation, which is the single most common electoral system in the world ("Table"). Moreover, alternative voting systems are already used in many elections throughout the United Kingdom, such as the elections of the Scottish Parliament, the Welsh Assembly and the Northern Ireland Assembly, the London Assembly and the Mayor of London, and local elections throughout Scotland and Northern Ireland. None of these jurisdictions have suffered from their electoral systems, and they have benefited from a number of advantages such as a range of minority views and a strong sense of voter enfranchisement and participation.

In summary, the "first past the post" election system used by the United Kingdom in electing its House of Commons is a clumsy and outdated system with a number of severe disadvantages. Many alternative systems are available that address these disadvantages to a greater or lesser degree, and these systems have been used throughout the world—and even within the borders of the United Kingdom—for generations without incident. The United Kingdom should reform its electoral system and improve democracy for all of its citizens.

Fukuzawa 8

Works Cited

Duverger, Maurice. *Party Politics and Pressure Groups: A Comparative Introduction*. Trans. David Wagoner. New York: Crowell, 1972. Print.

"Election 2010: Results." *BBC News*. 2010. Web. 20 Aug. 2011.

Gottlieb, Anthony. "Win or Lose." *The New Yorker*. 26 July 2010. Web. 20 Aug. 2011.

Loenen, Nick. *Citizenship and Democracy: A Case for Proportional Representation*. Toronto: Dundurn P, 1997. Print.

"Table of Electoral Systems Worldwide." *International IDEA*. International Institute for Democracy and Electoral Assistance. 2010. Web. 23 Aug. 2011.

> 新しいページから開始。論文中で引用した文献資料をアルファベット順に挙げる。論文で引用しなかった文献資料は含めない。

Appendix

1 エッセイ作成のスケジュール

日付	課題	メモ
	トピックを決める 文献資料調査	Chapter 4 を参考に。候補は？文献資料は豊富にあるか？
	Thesis を決める	Chapter 4 を参考に。
	リサーチをする	Chapter 5 を参考に。
	アウトラインを作成する	Chapter 4 を参考に。
	執筆	Chapters 1～7 を参考に。
	推敲 1	Chapter 7 を参考に。チェックリストの項目をすべて満たしているか確認。
	推敲 2	Chapter 7 を参考に。チェックリストの項目をすべて満たしているか確認。
	完成	Hurray!

2 ブレインストーミングのサンプル

　下の図はリストアップ方式の例です。"Blog" という題材をもとに、頭の中にある情報を書き出しています。頭に浮かんだままに書き出しているので、すべての情報間につながりがあるわけではありません。ブレインストーミングの段階では、有益かどうかといった判断はせずに、とにかく頭の中にある情報や思考をたぐり寄せ、紙の上に出すようにしましょう。この際、センテンスを作る必要はありません。深く考え込まずに、出てくるままにどんどん書き足していきます。

```
                    【Blog】

Internet            Design                       Political blog
Weblog              Reader                       Spread of news
Personal blog       Report (project, library, etc.)   Portability
Traditional diary   Speedy, handy                iPad, iPhone
Cooking recipes     Newspaper                    Copyright
Accessibility
```

　例えば 1,500 words 程度のエッセイを書く場合、ここに挙げた要素をすべて取り入れることはできません。ですが、このようにリストアップして自分の思考を客体化することで、"Blog" という全般的なテーマについて、自分はどのような側面について知っているのか、関心があるのか、また論を作成していく可能性があるのかが、よりはっきりと浮かび上がってきます。

　次に、ここでリストアップされた情報をグループ化してみます。すると、"Blog" の種類（Personal blog / Cooking recipes / Report / Political blog）、"Blog" とは対照的なもの（Traditional diary / Newspaper）、"Blog" の性質（Speedy, handy / Portability）、"Blog"

のアプリケーション関連(Design / iPad, iPhone)といったグループ化ができます。グループ同士で印をつけたり、線を引っ張ったりすることで、視覚的にも自分の思考内の整理をします。そうしたプロセスを経ることで、自分が特に焦点を当てたいと思う箇所や、論文として発展させることが可能そうな部分が、少しずつ見えてきます。

　上の例のように、扱う題材が論文のトピックとするのには大きすぎる場合は、このブレインストーミングを繰り返すことで、より具体的な内容へと絞り込むことができます。

3 エッセイの構想を練る

2を参考にして、実際にブレインストーミングをしてみましょう。

Topic ①

Topic 2

4 アウトライン

　議論の内容を明確にするために、箇条書き（例：小学校英語教育）ではなく、<u>文章形式</u>（例：小学校英語教育は教師不足が問題である）で記入しましょう。

<u>Basic Outline</u>

Topic:

Thesis Statement:

Detailed Outline

＊ Supporting points/body paragraphs の数は目安です。
＊ 引用する予定の文献資料も該当箇所に書き入れましょう。

Paragraph 1 (Introduction): Thesis Statement:

Paragraph 2: Main Idea:

Paragraph 3: Main Idea:

Paragraph 4: Main Idea:

Paragraph 5: Main Idea:

Paragraph 6: Main Idea:

Paragraph 7 (Conclusion):
Paraphrase of Thesis Statement:

5　文献資料記録ページ

＊このページを必要分コピーして、該当箇所に必要な情報を記入しましょう。

著者名：

タイトル：

文献の種類：書籍の章・新聞記事・雑誌記事・学術論文・Web・その他（　　　　）

タイトル：

文献の種類：書籍・新聞・雑誌・学術誌・Website・その他（　　　　）

編著者：

発行場所・発行者・発行年：

ページ：　　　～

概要：

引用したい箇所（引用符に入れ、ページ数も記入のこと）：

著者名：

タイトル：

文献の種類：書籍の章・新聞記事・雑誌記事・学術論文・Web・その他（　　　　）

タイトル：

文献の種類：書籍・新聞・雑誌・学術誌・Website・その他（　　　　）

編著者：

発行場所・発行者・発行年：

ページ：　　　　～

概要：

引用したい箇所（引用符に入れ、ページ数も記入のこと）：

6 チェックリスト

このリストを参照しながら推敲を行いましょう。すべての項目を満たしていますか？

Essay Checklist

	Formatting	
1	There is a margin on all four sides of the paper.	
2	The essay is double-spaced throughout.	
3	The font size is 12 points	
4	The title of the essay is centred on the first page of the essay. The title is appropriately capitalised.	
5	There is an indentation at the start of each paragraph.	
6	The author's family name and the page number are placed in the top right corner of each page, in line with the right edge of the body text.	
7	There is a period at the end of each sentence, followed by one space.	
8	The commas are followed by one space.	
	Academic Style	
1	There are no spelling errors and grammatical mistakes.	
2	The essay is written with vocabularies and expressions which are suitable for academic work.	

	Essay Structure	
1	The essay follows the outline and has introduction, body and conclusion.	
2	There is a clear thesis statement in the introduction.	
3	The conclusion restates the main idea of the essay and summarises the major supporting points.	
	Paragraph Structure	
1	The essay's argument is presented in a series of structured paragraphs.	
2	A paragraph contains one topic and one main idea.	
3	A paragraph has a topic sentence, which clearly states the main idea of the paragraph.	
	Coherence, Unity and Persuasiveness of Argument	
1	The topic is sufficiently narrow. The question to be addressed is clearly framed.	
2	The essay presents one unified argument/view about the question.	
3	There is unity and coherence throughout the essay.	
4	The logic of the argument is clearly indicated using transitional signals.	
5	The argument is supported by objective data such as examples, experts' opinions or statistics.	
6	There is a clear distinction between the author's own opinions and those of others.	
	Research: Use of Sources	
1	All the external materials are cited in MLA style, in the form of direct quotation, paraphrase, or summary.	
2	All the external materials are referenced in MLA style (in-text citations).	
3	All the external materials which are cited in the essay are listed in Works Cited, following MLA style.	

7 解答

CHAPTER 1

Practice 1 [*Sample answers*]
1. states, suggests, comments
2. run/operate/manage business

Practice 3 [*Sample answers*]
1. It is certain/highly likely that the event will be very successful.
2. Teenage children can be very sensitive to how they are perceived by their peers.
3. Children should be taught not to throw away/waste food.

CHAPTER 2

Practice 1
   (b)

Practice 2
1. Anti-piracy advertising campaigns on behalf of movie studios often equate breach of copyright with stealing, but this equivalence is open to question as a matter of both law and morality.
2. Two.
3. (a)

Review Exercises
1. [*Sample answers*]
   (a) This paragraph does not have a connecting argument. This list of characteristics could be connected together with opening and concluding statements such

as "The comic-book superhero has a number of well-defined characteristics" and "There are thousands of different superheroes in the Western comic-book tradition, but almost all of them conform to this basic pattern."

(b) This paragraph discusses more than one idea and none of them are satisfactorily developed.

(c) This is the best example of a paragraph.

2.

Topic sentence	h) There are three main characters that can be identified in William Shakespeare's sonnets.
Supporting point 1	f) The first is the Fair Youth, to whom the first 126 of the 154 sonnets are addressed.
Supporting detail 1	d) In these sonnets, the poet expresses a deep devotion to the young man in words and phrases that approach and even embrace the language of romantic love, with lyrical lines such as "Shall I compare thee to a summer's day?" (Sonnet 18) and "How like a winter hath my absence been | From thee" (Sonnet 97).
Supporting detail 2	a) The identity of the Fair Youth has been debated for centuries, but the question has never been settled.
Supporting point 2	g) Similarly, the Dark Lady of the second major sequence, sonnets 127 to 152, remains a mystery. These sonnets are more passionate and physical than the first group, suggesting an attachment that is explicitly sexual as well as emotional.

Supporting detail	b) The famous sonnet beginning "My mistress' eyes are nothing like the sun" (Sonnet 130) belongs firmly in this group.
Supporting point 3	c) The third character is identified as the Rival Poet, who appears in Sonnets 78 to 86.
Supporting detail	i) The Rival Poet competes with Shakespeare both for the love and attention of the Fair Youth, and for poetic achievement and artistic recognition.
Concluding sentence	e) Together, these three characters interact in fascinating ways to enrich the entire sequence of Shakespeare's sonnets.

3. [*Sample answers*]

    (a) The Hippocratic theory of bodily humours held that all diseases, disabilities and even temperaments resulted from an imbalance in the four basic substances present in the human body: black bile, yellow bile, phlegm and blood. **The first of these humours**, black bile, was thought to originate in the spleen. An excess of black bile would cause a person to become *melancholic*: that is, sad, withdrawn and even despondent. Many poets were thought to be melancholic. **In contrast**, **the second humour**, yellow bile, was produced by the gall bladder, and too much of it would make a person *choleric*, or angry, irritable and passionate. Military leaders and politicians were often described as choleric. **The third humour**, phlegm, came from the lungs. A surfeit of phlegm made a person *phlegmatic*, or passive, lethargic, and calm; a good administrator or civil servant might be thought of as phlegmatic. **The final humour**, blood, was produced in the liver but flowed through the arteries and veins. An excess of blood made a person *sanguine*: hopeful, courageous, and optimistic. A very sociable person with many friends, a perfect host or hostess, would be considered sanguine. By considering the proportions of these four humours in the body, physicians from ancient Greece to medieval England could diagnose every condition of the body and the mind.

(b)   Many lecturers in the UK feel that motivating their students is a bigger challenge today than decades ago. Most of the reasons are related to the change from an elitist to a mass higher education system. In the 1950s, only a small minority of the UK population participated in higher education, and they tended to stem from a relatively small, homogenous group. **However**, the background of students has become increasingly diverse with the rise in participation. **Necessarily** non-traditional students often feel excluded from institutions that are still dominantly white and middle-class, and this sense of exclusion could result in their lower motivation. **Furthermore**, the expansion of higher education has not led to a proportional increase in funding and facilities. **Consequently**, the student-lecturer ratio is higher than it was a generation ago. **Because of the lack of a personal relationship with lecturers**, students might feel they are treated as anonymous entities and become discouraged. **Thus**, motivating students from various backgrounds is now a major challenge facing the higher education system in the UK.

4. [*A sample answer*]

    Although video games are often seen as a distracting waste of time, they have important benefits that are only now being realised. Single-player video games can provide a sense of purpose, direction and optimism that extends into problems encountered in the real world. **They** can also enhance concentration, reaction time, spatial awareness and hand-eye coordination. **Multiplayer games** can promote cooperation and communication towards achieving a common goal, whether it be defending the world against aliens or working together in an office. **They can teach** general problem-solving techniques and even specific physical skills that may be useful in **players' lives or careers**; in fact, they are used extensively in military training and in professions from aviation to medicine. **Video games** can teach **people** to play the guitar, to drive a car or to play tennis better in the real world. **They** have also been developed to help solve difficult problems such as protein folding and effective financing in developing nations. To be sure, **video games** can be distracting and can even lead to physical and mental health problems if played to excess. Yet far from being worthless, **they have** many general and specific advantages that should not be overlooked.

5. [*A sample answer*]

A school uniform is sometimes viewed in a negative light, but it offers at least three benefits. Firstly, it helps parents financially by keeping the cost of clothing down. While it is true that the initial investment may not be insignificant, designs are simple and do not change, so school uniforms are reasonably priced and they do not need to be replaced every season. The second advantage of a school uniform is that it eases the peer pressure which many pupils feel at school. Teenagers are particularly conscious of how they look and how they are viewed by their peers. As a result, they tend to pay great attention to the clothes worn by others as well as by themselves. This can create tension and competitiveness among pupils, causing feelings of inferiority or superiority. If, however, everyone has to wear the same school uniform, the pupils have little control over what to wear and how they present themselves. The school uniform can thus reduce peer pressure related to clothes and appearance. Most importantly, a school uniform generates a sense of belonging in pupils because it embodies membership in the community of the school. Pupils wearing a uniform usually feel a stronger rapport with other pupils, teachers and staff members at school. They thus strive harder to achieve shared goals in areas such as academic performance; this leads them to make valuable contributions to the local community and to become actively involved in society as a whole. There are therefore several positive reasons for having a school uniform: it is effective in keeping the cost of clothing low and in easing peer pressure, and it helps the whole school to cohere and thrive as a community.

Chapter 5

Practice 1 [*A sample answer*]

Both science and religion are the source of deep beliefs about the origin and nature of the universe. However, only science tests itself through evidence and experiment, while the tenets of religion can never be proved or disproved. Because of this difference, it is wrong to say that science is a form of religion.

Practice 2 [*Sample answers*]

1. Whether motivation derives from within oneself or without determines how well one learns: an internally motivated person is likely to already possess an interest in the subject and to enjoy learning about it (Power 59-60).

2. It is not usual for someone whose motivation comes from outside to study a subject any more than is deemed necessary. However, an intrinsically motivated person is usually eager to learn and as a result often achieves an extensive knowledge of the subject.

3. The origin of motivation—whether it comes from within oneself or without—is one of the factors which determine our learning experience. First of all, people who gain motivation from within themselves tend to have an interest in the subject studied and find the experience rewarding. In contrast, externally motivated people are only driven by the prospect of tangible rewards, such as a good mark or a high-paying job. Consequently, the origin of motivation determines the extent of learning. Internally motivated people are keen on exploring the subject and are therefore more likely to have a more fulfilling learning experience. The lack of interest typical of externally motivated people, however, often results in a learning experience which is limited and less rewarding.

Chapter 6

Practice

1. (a)
2. (✓)
3. (c)
4. (e)
5. (d)
6. (d)
7. (b)
8. (✓)
9. (c)
10. (a)

Review Exercises

1

1. Topic: Political blog. Thesis statement: Although political blogs have had a significant effect on mainstream media, they have not replaced the need for traditional journalism.
2. It can be updated. . . . > They can be updated. . . .
   A political blog can provide. . . . > Political blogs can provide. . . .
   Most importantly, we can present. . . . > Most importantly, they can present. . . .
3. Five paragraphs.
4. (a) Political blogs have a number of advantages over the traditional mainstream media.
   (b) The mainstream media has reacted quickly to secure many of these advantages for itself.
   (c) Political bloggers have a number of important shortcomings when compared to the mainstream media.
   (d) It is difficult to see how the disadvantages faced by political blog sites can

be overcome.
5. (a) For example/For instance (b) However (c) As a result (d) For example/For instance
6. [*A sample answer*]

In conclusion, the political blog has several advantages over the mainstream media in freely and quickly spreading information and opinion that may otherwise be unavailable. It has had a significant and positive effect on the mainstream media. However, it continues to rely on the mainstream media for much of its primary content and has difficulty establishing and maintaining credibility. As a result, it is unlikely that the political blog can ever take the place of the mainstream media.

7. The Rise and Effect of the Political Blog on Mainstream Media
8. Gardner, Susannah, and Shane Birley. *Blogging for Dummies*. Hoboken: Wiley, 2008. Print.

MacMaster, Tom. "A Gay Girl in Damascus." *Blogspot.com*. Blogger, 19 Feb. 2011. Web. 7 July 2011.

Tremayne, Mark. "Harnessing the Active Audience: Synthesizing Blog Research and Lessons for the Future of Media." *Blogging, Citizenship, and the Future of Media*. Ed. Mark Tremayne. London: Routledge, 2007. 261-72. Print.

2 [*A sample answer*]

Outline

Title: The Rise and Effect of the Political Blog on Mainstream Media

I. Introduction

Thesis Statement: Although political blogs have had a significant effect on mainstream media, they have not replaced the need for traditional journalism.

II. Body

    A. Political blogs have a number of advantages over the traditional mainstream media.

        1. They are cheaply and easily accessible.

2. They are continuously and flexibly updated.
3. They provide information and opinion that may not be available in the mainstream media.
4. They provide eyewitness accounts from people on the ground.
- **B.** The mainstream media has adapted to secure these advantages for itself.
    1. Most newspapers now have online versions.
    2. Many online newspapers now have blog sections linked to a range of other sources.
- **C.** Political blogs have a number of shortcomings when compared to mainstream media.
    1. They do not have the resources for much original investigative journalism.
        a. Travel.
        b. Press credentials.
        c. Contacts and reputation.
    2. They rely on the mainstream media for primary materials.
        a. Most links in blog posts are to mainstream media.
        b. Most blog posts consist of analysis or opinion rather than factual reporting.
    3. They have limited credibility.
        a. They are not as accountable as the commercial media.
        b. They are often anonymous or pseudonymous.
- **D.** It is not clear that bloggers can overcome these shortcomings.
    1. Limited access to revenues.
    2. Limited ability to coordinate.
    3. Limited institutional reputation.

III. Conclusion

Chapter 7

Practice

1. The change in the national curriculum in 1992 marked "a definitive turning point" (Baker 88).
2. One critic concludes, "It was one of her earliest poems, 'After the Worst' that testifies to her extraordinary visual imagination" (Springfield 5).
3. Everyone was fascinated when Mr Obama, a presidential candidate at that time, exclaimed, "Change."
4. According to an article in *Asahi Shimbun*, scientists have found evidence that a lack of sleep is one of the contributing factors for weight gain.
5. The article raises the question, "Is it really necessary to teach English at primary school?" This uncertainty is shared by many who work in primary school education.

迫　桂（さこ　かつら）
略　　歴：英国ウォリック大学大学院英語比較文学科博士課程修了(PhD in English and Comparative Literary Studies)。現在、慶應義塾大学経済学部教授。
専　　攻：戦後・現代イギリス文学
主な業績：*Contemporary Narratives of Dementia: Ethics, Ageing, Politics.* Routledge, 2019（共著）、ほか

徳永聡子（とくなが　さとこ）
略　　歴：慶應義塾大学大学院文学研究科博士課程修了（文学博士）。現在、慶應義塾大学文学部教授。
専　　攻：中世イギリス文学、書誌学
主な業績：*Caxton's Golden Legend*, vol. 1. Oxford University Press, 2020（共編著）、ほか

英語論文の書き方入門

2012 年 4 月 20 日　初版第 1 刷発行
2021 年 4 月 1 日　初版第 6 刷発行

著　者―――迫　桂・徳永聡子
発行者―――依田俊之
発行所―――慶應義塾大学出版会株式会社
　　　　　　〒108-8346　東京都港区三田 2-19-30
　　　　　　TEL　〔編集部〕03-3451-0931
　　　　　　　　 〔営業部〕03-3451-3584〈ご注文〉
　　　　　　　　 〔　〃　〕03-3451-6926
　　　　　　FAX　〔営業部〕03-3451-3122
　　　　　　振替　00190-8-155497
　　　　　　https://www.keio-up.co.jp/
本文 DTP 装丁―土屋　光
印刷・製本―――中央精版印刷株式会社
カバー印刷―――株式会社太平印刷社

　　　　　　ⓒ 2012 Katsura Sako, Satoko Tokunaga
　　　　　　Printed in Japan ISBN978-4-7664-1921-4